NATURE'S FURY

Eyewitness Reports of Natural Disasters

CAROLE GARBUNY VOGEL

SCHOLASTIC REFERENCE

To my nieces and nephews: Sarah, Rachel, and Jim Prunier; Dan, Brian, and Adam Butterworth; and Emily and Zachary Best, and for Audrey Davis, who may as well be a niece as she is such an important part of my family.

The account describing Anne T. Donaghy's experiences during the 1964 Good Friday Earthquake on pages 21–22 is used by permission.

The account describing Mike and Lu Moore's experiences on Mount St. Helens that appears on pages 39–40 is used by permission.

Isaac Cline's account of the 1900 Galveston Hurricane, which appears on pages 45, 46, 47, and 48, is from STORMS, FLOODS AND SUNSHINE: A BOOK OF MEMOIRS by Isaac Monroe Cline © 1945 and used by permission of the licensor, Pelican Publishing Company, Inc.

Edith Anderson's experiences during the New England Hurricane of 1938, recounted on pages 54 and 57, are taken from "The Hurricane of 1938—Edith Anderson's Story," transcribed by Donald West (91989), in the Albert T. Klyberg Collection. Courtesy of the Manuscript Collection, Rhode Island Historical Society.

Text excerpts on pages 75, and 78–79 appear courtesy of The New-York Historical Society.

Caroline Henderson's description of life in the Dust Bowl region, included on pages 92 and 94–95, are from "Dust to Eat," by Caroline A. Henderson in *The Chronicles of Oklahoma,* Vol. LVIII, No. 4, Winter 1980–1981. Copyright © 1981 Oklahoma Historical Society. Used by permission.

Every effort has been made by the publisher to locate owners of the copyrighted material reprinted in this book and to secure the necessary permissions. If there are any questions regarding the use of these materials, the publisher will take appropriate corrective measures to acknowledge ownership in future editions.

CONSULTANT: Jonathan D. W. Kahl, Associate Professor, Atmospheric Sciences, University of Wisconsin-Milwaukee.

ISBN 0-439-25966-5

Copyright © 2000 by Carole Garbuny Vogel.
All rights reserved.
Published by Scholastic Inc.
SCHOLASTIC and associated logos are trademarks and/or registered trademarks of Scholastic Inc.

12 11 10 9 8 7 6 5 4 3 2 1   0 1 2 3 4 5/0

Printed in the U.S.A.   09

First Scholastic paperback printing, October 2000

Book design by Nancy Sabato   Composition by Brad Walrod   Map art by Paul Colin

Table of Contents

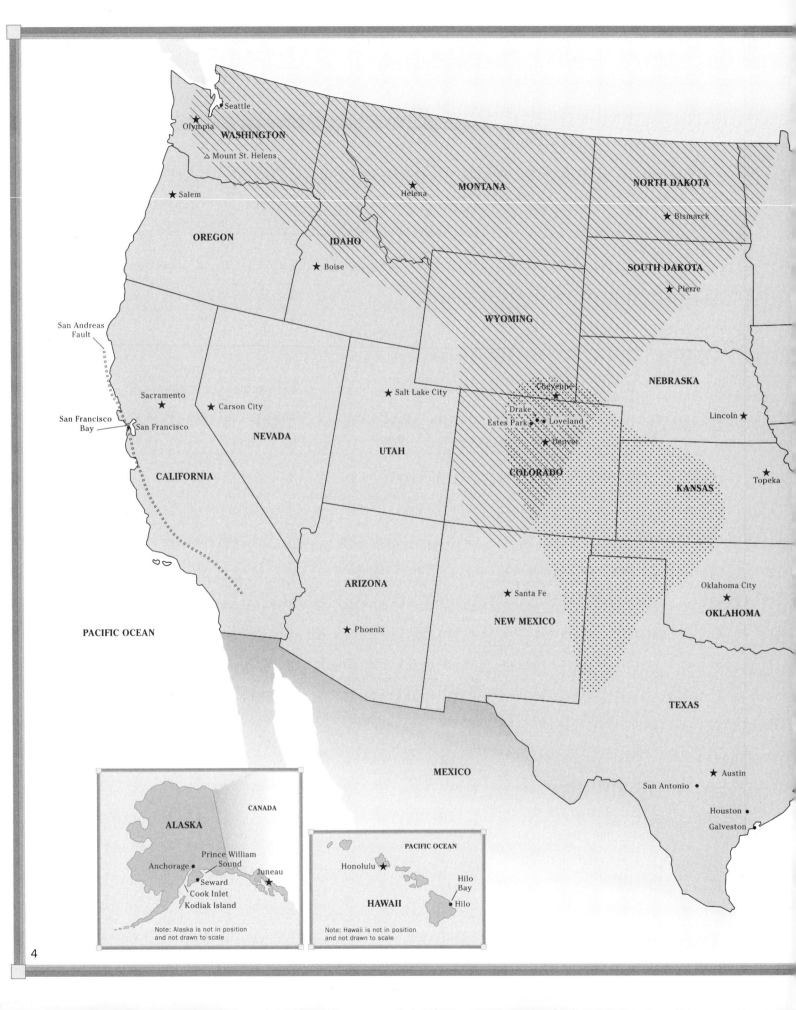

Seattle ★

Olympia •

WASHINGTON

△ Mount St. Helens

Salem ★

OREGON

MONTANA

Helena ★

NORTH DAKOTA

Bismarck ★

Boise ★

IDAHO

SOUTH DAKOTA

Pierre ★

WYOMING

San Andreas Fault

Sacramento ★

Carson City ★

Salt Lake City ★

Cheyenne ★

NEBRASKA

Lincoln ★

San Francisco Bay

San Francisco

Drake •

Estes Park • • Loveland

Denver ★

NEVADA

UTAH

COLORADO

Topeka ★

CALIFORNIA

KANSAS

PACIFIC OCEAN

ARIZONA

Santa Fe ★

Oklahoma City ★

Phoenix ★

NEW MEXICO

OKLAHOMA

TEXAS

MEXICO

Austin ★

San Antonio •

Houston •

Galveston •

CANADA

ALASKA

Prince William Sound

Anchorage •

Seward •

Juneau ★

Cook Inlet

Kodiak Island

Note: Alaska is not in position and not drawn to scale

PACIFIC OCEAN

Honolulu ★

Hilo Bay

Hilo •

HAWAII

Note: Hawaii is not in position and not drawn to scale

CANADA

Note: Peshtigo fire area is not in position and not drawn to scale

Menomonee •
Peshtigo •
Green Bay
Green Bay •
Lake Michigan
WISCONSIN

• Ontario

MINNESOTA

Lake Superior

MICHIGAN

Menomonee •
Peshtigo •
Green Bay

★ St. Paul

WISCONSIN

Madison ★

Lake Michigan

Lake Huron

MICHIGAN

Lansing •

IOWA

Des Moines ★

Chicago •

ILLINOIS

INDIANA

Indianapolis ★

Springfield ★

Lake Ontario

Buffalo •

Lake Erie

PENNSYLVANIA

Harrisburg ★

OHIO

Columbus ★

Xenia •

MISSOURI

Jefferson City ★

Princeton •

DeSoto •
Murphysboro •

Poplar Bluff •

KENTUCKY

Frankfort ★

WEST VIRGINIA

Charleston ★

Richmond ★

VIRGINIA

Washington D.C. ⊛

ARKANSAS

Little Rock ★

Nashville ★

TENNESSEE

NORTH CAROLINA

Raleigh ★

ATLANTIC OCEAN

MAINE

Augusta ★

VERMONT

Montpelier ★

NEW YORK

Albany ★

Concord ★ **NEW HAMPSHIRE**

Boston ★ **MASSACHUSETTS**

Hartford ★

Providence

RHODE ISLAND

CONNECTICUT

New Haven

Long Island Sound

Long Island

New York City

Trenton ★

NEW JERSEY

Dover ★ **DELAWARE**

MARYLAND

Annapolis

MISSISSIPPI

Jackson ★

ALABAMA

Montgomery ★

GEORGIA

Atlanta •

Columbia ★

SOUTH CAROLINA

LOUISIANA

Baton Rouge ★

Tallahassee ★

FLORIDA

TEXAS

Galveston •

GULF OF MEXICO

Note: Galveston area is not in position and not drawn to scale

GULF OF MEXICO

LEGEND

1974 Tornado Outbreak

Blizzard of 1888

Dust Bowl

Peshtigo Fire area

Mount St. Helens ash fall area (Most areas beyond western Montana received only trace amounts of ash.)

★ State Capital

⊛ National Capital

Miles
0   100   200   300   400

200   400   600
Kilometers

Author's Note

My friends and colleagues call me the "Queen of Natural Disasters" because I love to write about nature in all her fury. My sixth-grade teacher sparked my interest in disasters when she shared a *National Geographic* article on the ancient Roman city, Pompeii, with the class. An eruption of Mount Vesuvius in AD 79 had buried Pompeii in a thick layer of ash and cinders. In modern times archeologists excavated the city, revealing the forms of the victims killed by the eruption. I was fascinated by the images of people frozen in motion and from that point on I was hooked.

Our restless planet gives me plenty of material to write about—volcanoes, earthquakes, tornadoes, tsunamis, hurricanes, floods, and fires. Sometimes the losses resulting from these events are small—fallen trees, disruptions in power. At other times, the losses are staggering—whole towns or cities destroyed. Yet from such catastrophes emerge stories of stunning human resilience, of suffering overcome by courage, ingenuity, stamina, and luck. These are the stories that fascinate me. I want to know more about how people survive against tremendous odds.

This book tells the dramatic stories of thirteen natural disasters. It investigates what caused them and how people survived them. What makes the book special is that the survivors describe their experiences in their own words. The challenge of writing it was in obtaining eyewitness accounts that were clear and compelling, and that would grab the attention of young people.

I became an amateur detective, employing the same techniques a private eye uses to track down missing people. I focused on three main sources of eyewitness testimony:

- survivors I interviewed
- letters, diaries, and transcripts in historical societies and libraries
- old newspapers and magazines with first-person accounts.

I began my search in my local library, then branched out to libraries and historical societies across the country, contacting them by phone, fax, or e-mail.

Initially, I thought getting eyewitness testimonies would be the easiest part of the research. I would use published accounts to identify the people I was interested in and then I would track them down through phone books. However, all of the people

I wanted to talk to had survived disasters that had taken place 20 years ago or more. The only person for whom my plan worked was Jerry Aqualina, curator of the Buffalo Zoo. I came across his story in *White Death: Blizzard of '77* by Erno Rossi, which described a catastrophic blizzard that had struck Buffalo, New York, in 1977. The book included a section about Mr. Aqualina's phenomenal efforts to get the zoo animals fed and to prevent them from escaping. Lucky for me, Mr. Aqualina still worked at the zoo and was willing to be interviewed. His story appears on pages 86–88.

To round out my chapter on the Buffalo Blizzard, I telephoned the public relations office of the Buffalo Police Department. I asked if there were any officers on the force who had participated in rescues during the storm. That's how I found Chief Larry Ramunno, whose heroics are recorded on pages 84–85.

The Good Friday Earthquake roared through Alaska in 1964 and inflicted severe damage on the city of Anchorage. So I contacted the Anchorage Museum of History and Art and asked archivist Diane Brenner if she knew any quake survivors who had been kids at the time of the disaster. Ms. Brenner referred me to Sharon Abbott, the museum's curator of education, who in turn referred me to Bob Lloyd. I interviewed Mr. Lloyd by phone, and his story appears on page 20.

I came across an article by Tay Pryor Thomas in the July 1964 issue of *National Geographic* magazine. In the article Mrs. Thomas describes the terror she and her children, Anne and Dave, had experienced when their house collapsed and plunged over a cliff during the Good Friday Earthquake. I couldn't find Mrs. Thomas in the Anchorage phone directory. But another associate of Ms. Brenner—Jim Gottstein—helped me reach Dave Thomas in Alaska. Mr. Thomas connected me with his sister Anne in New Hampshire. You can read Anne's amazing account on pages 21–23.

While researching the Great Flash Flood of Big Thompson Canyon in Colorado, I learned that many people had escaped the raging waters by climbing the steep rock walls of the canyon, finding refuge on narrow ledges. One account stated that survivors had to share this high ground with thousands of rattlesnakes that had escaped the rising water. Now this was a story I wanted to share with my readers! But I couldn't find any other mention of rattlesnakes, except one about a pet goat that had been bitten by a rattler the day of the flood.

Looking for more details, I called the Larimer County Sheriff's Department in Colorado, where I was referred to two people who had been active in the rescue effort. Neither had heard of any human encounters with rattlesnakes during the flood, but one of my contacts suggested that I speak with John Lippert, a deputy sheriff who had survived the flood by scaling the canyon walls. Unfortunately, he quashed the rattlesnake angle, but he provided me with a thrilling description of his own adventure, which is detailed on pages 107–108 and 111.

I was disappointed that I couldn't use the rattlesnake story, but I know that some students use my books as references for reports. Therefore, I have a responsibility to verify my information and make my writing as accurate as possible.

During the time I was contacting survivors, I was also speaking in schools. In my talks I tried to show students what professional writers of nonfiction have in common with student authors.

At the end of one talk, a girl asked me, "Why do you write mainly about disasters?"

"Because they interest me," I replied.

"You must be really sick," she said. "Only a sick person would spend so much time on such a morbid topic."

I left the school wondering if my books really were just morbid accounts. But the very next day I interviewed Betty Nelson, an Alaskan woman whose seaside village had been severely damaged by a tsunami. She told me that before the tsunami struck, the water had drained out of the bay, exposing rocks on the seafloor that she had never seen before.

"Normally I would have been tempted to go out and explore," she said. "But I had once read about how people in Hawaii had dashed out to pick up fish and shells when the same thing happened there. These people drowned when a giant wave rushed in and reclaimed the bay."

What a marvelous thing to hear! Books about disasters are not just morbid tales. They really save lives. You can read Mrs. Nelson's account on pages 24–25.

For me, the stories in this book show that the power of the human spirit is equal to the unexpected challenges that nature presents. I hope you find them as compelling as I did.

Carole G. Vogel
Lexington, Massachusetts
April 9, 1999

PART 1

On Shaky Ground

Although the ground beneath our feet feels solid and reliable, the earth's rigid crust is just a thin skin encasing a hot, molten planet. It is this molten underpinning that is responsible for Earth's volcanoes and most of its earthquakes.

If you could dig through the crust and travel to the center of the earth, you would notice that the deeper you tunneled the hotter the rock around you becomes. The earth's core is as hot as the surface of the sun, and it acts like a furnace without an off switch. Heat from the core continually heats the mantle layer above it, causing a never-ending flow of molten rock within the mantle. Columns of hot rock slowly rise from the bottom of the mantle, spread out at the top, and push the cooler rock out of the way. The cooler rock sinks down into the mantle where it is reheated and rises again.

The earth's crust floats on top of the mantle. The crust is broken into separate sections called plates, which carry the continents and the ocean floor. Like the pieces of a cracked eggshell, the plates fit closely together along jagged edges. The flow of hot rock in the mantle can pull plates apart, push plates together, or grind plates past each other. The interaction of plates at their boundaries may unleash earthquakes and volcanoes, creating chaos on the surface of the earth.

Where two plates scrape past each other, earthquakes frequently occur. Where plates move apart, volcanoes form, gushing out lava. The lava hardens and creates a ribbon of new crust that welds itself to the edges of the plates. The new crust temporarily patches the plates together. The "patch" holds until the next stream of lava gurgles up between the plates. This process formed the Mid-Ocean Ridge, a 46,000-mile-long (73,600 km) underwater mountain system that extends into all oceans.

Where two plates with continents collide, they buckle the crust, setting off earthquakes. This process raises the land into mighty mountain ranges like the Himalayas. If a plate lugging ocean floor slams into another, or into a continent-carrying plate, it dives under the other plate into a deep underwater canyon called a deep-ocean trench. Usually molten rock from the descending melting plate collects below the surface, slowly raising the land overhead and occasionally setting off major earthquakes.

Sometimes, the molten rock breaks through the surface of the overriding plate and creates a chain of volcanoes. This is happening along the Ring of Fire, a belt of volcanoes that rims the Pacific Ocean, and along the Mediterranean Belt, a series of volcanoes that stretches eastward from the Mediterranean Sea to Indonesia. Together these two belts account for most of the world's active volcanoes that erupt on land, and for the majority of Earth's most damaging earthquakes.

The same tectonic plate motions that produce earthquakes and volcanoes can also give rise to tsunamis. If the plate movement is powerful enough and if it occurs offshore, it can violently raise or lower a large section of the seafloor. As the ocean bottom moves, it pushes water out of its way. The water has to go somewhere, just as water in a bathtub has to go somewhere when someone sloshes swiftly back and forth. In the ocean the water turns into tsunamis that spread out and speed across the sea.

In the open ocean, tsunamis rise only two feet or so above the normal wave height. But as they approach shallow water near a coastline, they grow. Some tsunamis strike land as a wall of water, but most appear as a swiftly rising tide that keeps on going. Tsunamis travel at incredible speeds, often greater than 500 miles (800 km) per hour.

Although geologists know what causes earthquakes, volcanic eruptions, and tsunamis, they cannot prevent them. Occasionally, big earthquakes give a clear warning weeks, days, or hours before they hit. The water level in wells may change dramatically. Animals may act strangely. And a series of little quakes—foreshocks—may jiggle the area. More often than not, however, the signs of an impending earthquake are more subtle. They usually consist of a slight rise or fall in the elevation and tilt of the landscape. These changes cannot be detected by direct observation because they happen too slowly.

However, geologists using a variety of instruments, including satellites with special sensors, can measure changes in the earth's crust. Someday geologists may be able to interpret these changes well enough that they can provide an early warning to nearby populations. The ability to predict earthquakes will come none too soon for the residents of California and other earthquake-prone regions.

The Great San Francisco Earthquake

California is perched atop the San Andreas Fault, the boundary between the North American plate, which carries most of North America, and the Pacific plate, which supports the Pacific Ocean and a sliver of North America. When the plates wrench past each other, they rip open a segment of the fault, unleashing an earthquake. The shifting plates make California prime earthquake territory. But so far geologists have had no success in predicting exactly when and where the quakes will strike.

One of the most destructive earthquakes in California's history began at 5:12 AM on April 18, 1906, about 8 miles (13 km) west of where San Francisco's Golden Gate Bridge

A fissure caused by the San Francisco earthquake of 1906 ripped apart the cobblestone pavement on East Street.

now stands. The Pacific plate lurched as much as 28 feet (8.5 m) northward along a 290-mile-long (464 km) segment of the fault. The resulting earthquake jolted awake the residents of northern California.

In San Francisco, the ground rolled up and down for 40 seconds like waves on an ocean. Ten seconds of quiet followed. Then an even more powerful tremor ripped through the city. For another agonizing 45 to 60 seconds, strong shaking punctuated with violent shocks rocked the metropolis. The temblor had a moment-magnitude of 7.9, making it one of the most powerful earthquakes to hit California.

The moment-magnitude scale is a rating system that estimates the total energy released during an earthquake. Earthquakes below 5.0 on the moment-magnitude scale are small and produce little destruction. Those above 5.0 can inflict great damage, especially when they strike near or below large cities like San Francisco.

The violent shaking reduced thousands of buildings to rubble. Fissures split open streets. Uprooted streetcar tracks lay twisted on the pavement. The cries of those trapped and injured by the falling debris instigated rescue efforts. For some, however, help would never come.

W.E. Alexander and his wife and children were among the lucky ones. The sturdy design of their well-constructed apartment building probably saved their lives. Alexander sent this account of the earthquake to his cousin:

> "I was shaken in every direction, shaken until I thought my teeth would come out."

"I was in bed at the time and did not get out until the shake was over. My feelings were like what I suppose a rat's are when vigorously shaken by a terrier and then slammed down on the ground. I was shaken in every direction, shaken until I thought my teeth would come out. The bed jumped up and down and sideways and at last it hit the floor with a harder and more vicious jam than any of the others, as if to say, 'Now I've got you.'

"...the glassware, plaques, pictures, bottles, etc. were crashing to the floors and creating a din that was not reassuring. We were on the second floor of a very well-built five-story wooden apartment house...I expected every moment that the three stories above us would come crashing through the ceilings and cover us under a ton of debris, or the whole building [would] break loose and roll down the hill....

"We ran to the windows and saw that the streets were full of people who looked like

frenzied ants whose home had been stirred up with a stick. They were bare-footed and in all stages of reckless dishabille, treading around on broken glass and brickbats, trying to find out what had hit them, and I never felt so small and helpless in my life as I did that morning when I gazed upon the stricken city."[1]

Within moments of the earthquake, about 50 fires erupted within the city, sparked by broken gas and electrical lines, as well as by hot coals spilled from upended stoves. Water gushed from shattered water mains, rendering it useless for firefighting. The small fires soon converged into one large conflagration. Without water, the only way to fight the firestorm was with destruction. By dynamiting buildings in the path of the flames, firefighters hoped to create a gap that the flames could not cross. But time and again the fire leaped over the dynamited ruins. By 5:00 PM, 12 hours after the quake struck, half the city lay in a smoldering heap.

The fire raged through the night. The ground shook from aftershocks and dynamiting. When the fire was finally extinguished on the third day, 28,188 buildings had been lost and 514 city blocks in a 4-square-mile area (10 sq. km) had gone up in smoke. Of San Francisco's 400,000 residents, more than 3,000 were dead and approximately 225,000 were homeless.

Two months later, on July 20, 1906, Carrie A. Mangels wrote of her experiences in a letter to her uncle: "... Even after seeing how the fire was gaining we still had hopes. In fact everybody did. But now we wonder how we could have entertained any hopes when we knew that the water mains were broken and that the firemen had nothing with which to fight the fire. The soldiers dynamited different buildings to check the flames but instead of stopping them, it made matters worse....

"The sidewalks were covered with men, women, and children. In one place we saw a mother who had her children wrapt in blankets and kept watch over them and the few things she had saved. Some less fortunate ones had to sleep on the cold streets, some leaned against fences and slept that way; others lay on the sidewalks. They were so worn-out it did not matter to them.

"In the meantime a proclamation had been issued by the Mayor that martial law had been declared and that anybody caught looting would be shot....

San Francisco residents watch spellbound as fire engulfs the heart of their city and spreads outward.

Army troops march past the remains of the Hotel California in San Francisco. Soldiers had orders to enforce the strict curfew, shoot looters, and obtain food for the hungry citizens.

"For about a week the City was in total darkness every night. Everybody had to be in the house by eight o'clock. Anybody out after that time was challenged by soldiers and if they did not halt were liable to be shot....

"After a week or so lights were allowed till eight o'clock. No coal-oil lamps, just candles. Almost every chimney was down and cooking was done in the streets. People cooked out of doors for about two months. They took their stoves in the street and built little houses around them....

"The people would walk for blocks in order to get drinking water. Some houses had water and some didn't. When it did run, it was dirty and smelt bad.

"For about one week there were no stores opened at all, Money was no good then. If we wanted anything to eat we had to go to the Relief Stations and get rations. They gave us canned goods, potatoes, flour, coffee, bread, soda-crackers, and some days, meat. The first few days all the grocery stores were raided by the soldiers so as to get food for the people and then relief trains came in from all over the country." [2]

All but one of San Francisco's banks had burned with their money locked inside their vaults. The exception was the small Bank of Italy, whose president, Amadeo Peter Giannini, had rescued the bank's cash reserve of $80,000. Using a board supported by two barrels, Giannini began lending money to San Franciscans who wanted to rebuild the city. From this small rebirth, Giannini's bank eventually became the powerful Bank of America.

San Francisco needed more cash for reconstruction than one

Earthquake survivors, whose homes were destroyed or damaged, crowded into city parks and set up temporary shelters.

bank could provide. But executives of large corporations with business interests in San Francisco worried that moneylenders from the East Coast would not invest in their earthquake-prone city. So they began a campaign to have the catastrophe called a fire instead of an earthquake. Photographs released to the press were retouched to remove evidence of earthquake damage. In that era, conflagrations posed a major threat to all cities so they were not considered an unusual risk to investors.

Money soon poured in from other parts of the country, and the cleanup and rebuilding of San Francisco began. Within a week, many businesses set up shop in some of the large houses spared from the flames. Crews working around the clock cleared the debris and deposited most of it off the shoreline of San Francisco. In the following two months more than 8,000 barracks were built to house the homeless. By the end of three years, nearly 20,000 permanent homes had been constructed. Nine years after the disaster, San Francisco had recovered enough to successfully host a World's Fair. The new buildings of San Francisco were stronger than the ones they replaced because the city planners wanted to minimize damage from future quakes.

Survivors wait in line for government aid and supplies at a relief station near St. Mary's Cathedral. Even those with money in their pockets found that there were no stores left to spend it in.

But the planners made a major mistake.

So much rubble had been dumped during the cleanup that it filled in portions of San Francisco Bay. City planners allowed the landfill to become the foundation for new neighborhoods such as the Marina District. Unfortunately, landfill becomes unstable during the intense shaking caused by earthquakes, and buildings placed on top of it are prone to collapse. By building atop the landfill, San Francisco set the stage for future catastrophes. The consequences of building on landfill became apparent in 1989 during the Loma Prieta earthquake. The temblor, named for a mountain peak near its epicenter in the Santa Cruz Mountains south of San Francisco, severely damaged 200 buildings in the Marina District. Fires fed by ruptured gas lines erupted there. However, minimal winds, and a prompt response from firefighters and concerned citizens, prevented the blazes from spreading as they had in the aftermath of the 1906 quake.

Like California, Alaska is prone to earthquakes. The residents of Anchorage would see their city torn apart in the early spring of 1964.

CHAPTER 2

Alaska's Good Friday Earthquake

In the late afternoon of Good Friday, March 27, 1964, shoppers, pedestrians, and motorists stuck in rush-hour traffic filled the downtown business district of Anchorage, Alaska's largest city. Suddenly, the pavement began to heave in great rolling waves. Buildings wobbled and some crumbled. Roads were split by gaping fissures. Terrified, people clung to each other and to lampposts.

This seismic event, known as the Good Friday Earthquake, measured 9.2 on the moment-magnitude scale, and lasted an amazing four minutes. It was the most powerful temblor to strike the western coast of North America in historic times.

The March 27 earthquake shifted this segment of Fourth Avenue—the main road in Anchorage—about 20 feet (6 m) below street level.

19

Bob Lloyd was 12 years old in 1964 and accustomed to the minor temblors that shook his home every so often. But he will never forget this one. In a phone interview 33 years later, Bob described what happened: "I was sitting at the dinner table with my father and sister. Mom brought out the main course—liver—and I began to hope against hope that God would save me. Suddenly the room began to shake.

"Although the earthquake started like previous quakes I had experienced, within a few moments I knew this one was different. I heard the quake coming. It made a low growling sound that got louder and built up to a gigantic roar. The dishes rattled and the chandelier swayed. I thought the shaking would stop but it kept growing stronger. Dad yelled, 'Get out of the house!'

"We raced outside and clung to our split-rail fence. I noticed that our car was 'walking' down the driveway. The driveway was nearly flat with a slight slope toward the street. When the car reached the end of the driveway it seemed to defy gravity and rolled back up.

"I looked down the street and I saw the pavement ripple like waves on the surface of a lake. The utility poles bobbed back and forth, causing the wires to stretch and then loosen. Near our house an electrical transformer exploded, sending out a shower of sparks.

"The loud rumbling continued throughout the quake. It sounded like a big freight train rolling by. I was awestruck and scared. I knew that nothing I could do would affect what was happening.

"After five minutes or so, the shaking stopped and we went back inside. Amazingly, little damage had occurred. The walls were cracked and the contents of the kitchen cupboards had tumbled onto the floor and counters. I couldn't help thinking that my prayers had been answered when I reached the dining room. My dinner had fallen off the table and our dog had scarfed it up!"[1]

The earthquake originated about 12 miles (19 km) underground, beneath the shore of Prince William Sound, 80 miles (128 km) southeast of Anchorage and 120 miles (192 km) west of Seward. Releasing at least twice the energy of the 1906 San Francisco Earthquake, the temblor dramatically impacted an area 500 miles (800 km) long and 150 miles (240 km) wide. Shock waves sped out in all directions, roaring

> "It made a low growling sound that got louder and built up to a gigantic roar."

through south central Alaska and triggering landslides and avalanches.

The Anchorage home of 8-year-old Anne Thomas was destroyed in one of the land-slides. Anne lived with her parents and 6-year-old brother Dave in a split-level house on the top of a steep bluff overlooking Cook Inlet. Quick thinking on their mother's part saved the lives of Anne and Dave. Their father was away when the earthquake struck.

Like Bob Lloyd, Anne Thomas Donaghy remember-ed hearing a deep rumbling sound first. She recalled the speed with which her mother reacted: "Mom jumped up

Gaping black cracks appeared in the snow where fissures opened during the earthquake. Homes and buildings perched atop these crevasses were seriously damaged.

right away and said, 'It's an earthquake. Come with me!' Dave and I raced downstairs after my mom. The whole house was shaking harder than it had ever shook before. Mom opened the front door and ordered us outside, even though it was snowy and I was in socks and my brother was barefoot. The two of us were wearing just T-shirts and jeans. Mom didn't have any shoes on, either.

"We dashed out to the snowy yard, but the shaking was so fierce that it flung us to the ground. Suddenly black lines started running through the snow in every direction. I realized that the lines were cracks forming in the dark dirt below the snow. As the quake heaved the ground up and down, the cracks grew bigger and bigger. The little plot of snow-covered lawn we were on became a small island surrounded by enor-mous dark fissures that opened up all around us. As our island jolted up and down, it tilted sharply. We dug our fingers down into the snow to hold on. A crack started open-ing between my mom and me and she quickly pulled me across. Dave began to cry.

Eight-year-old Anne Thomas and her family survived the Good Friday Earthquake, but their home was demolished.

"I heard glass smashing and the screech of our wooden house being pulled apart. I never saw it though. My head was turned the other way. I watched tall pine trees at one end of our yard whip back and forth until their black roots pulled right out of the snow. Our swing set zipped past us on its own little island, and we never saw it again. I had this strange falling feeling in the pit of my stomach, like you get on a Ferris wheel.

"Finally all the shaking and terrible noise stopped. After all of the rumbling and smashing and crashing, the silence was the loudest thing imaginable. Dave stopped crying to listen. Then the three of us all turned to look behind us and had quite a shock: A huge black cliff stood there, where our driveway had once been. Broken pipes stuck out of the black earth, with water trickling out of them. I realized that our house had been up there, and during the earthquake we had slid with it all the way down to the shore of the gray inlet, a drop of about 300 feet [90 m].

"Now we were in a crazy quilt of uprooted trees, downed power lines, and slabs of dirt tilted at strange angles. What once was a home, front yard, and driveway was now just a jumble of dirt, debris, and dangerous crevasses.

"Mom kept saying, 'We have to get out of here!' Later she told me she was worried about a tidal wave coming in. It took us about twenty minutes to scramble over this dangerous terrain and reach the base of the cliff. We were quite cold by then and had lost the feeling in our feet. Some people were up there, looking down at us. A man quickly slid and stumbled down a gentler part of the cliff. He put his heavy gray wool coat around my shoulders and it seemed like one of the nicest things a person had ever done for me. Then he carried Dave up on his back. When we reached the top, we were led to a car with the heater running, and we started to warm up. None of us got frostbite, even though we had been in the snow and cold for so long."[2]

The quake destroyed Anne Thomas's neighborhood, the Turnagain area of Anchorage.

At about the same time that the Thomas house collapsed, the initial shock waves reached the port city of Seward. The shaking caused a tremendous landslide along the city's waterfront. Piers, warehouses, and oil storage tanks plunged into the bay. The tanks exploded and spewed flaming petroleum onto the wreckage. Then a three-story wave produced by the landslide slammed into the city. The wave washed ashore the slick of burning debris. More giant waves followed. Seward did not stand a chance against the triple threat of quake, fire, and harbor waves. Although the calamity quickly reduced the city to ruins, only 12 people perished.

The earthquake had thrust vast areas of the seafloor upward by as much as 38 feet (11.5 m), displacing enormous amounts of seawater and setting tsunamis—giant waves—in motion. Like a titanic battering ram, the tsunamis crashed into the settlements along Alaska's coast. The tsunamis caused more devastation in some places than the temblor itself.

Tsunamis, landslides, and fires caused by the 1964 earthquake wreaked havoc on the city of Seward, Alaska.

Like Anne Thomas's mother, Betty Nelson helped save her family. Her home on an island along the Alaskan coast lay directly in the path of the tsunamis generated by the Good Friday Earthquake. In a phone conversation more than 33 years later, Mrs. Nelson recalled what happened after the quake:

"My husband Abner and I had built a ten-room house in a small fishing village on Afognak Island, north of Kodiak Island. The house was on the beach. We were living there with three of our children at the time of the earthquake. Our oldest child was away at college.

"About fifteen minutes after the earthquake struck I was looking out the window. I saw the water drain from the bay as if a giant vacuum cleaner was sucking it up. On the newly exposed seafloor lay rocks that I had never seen before. Normally, I would have been tempted to go out and explore. But I had once read about how people in Hawaii had dashed out to pick up fish and shells when the same thing happened there. These people drowned when a giant wave rushed in and reclaimed the bay.

"I yelled to Abner that we needed to flee to high ground immediately. I grabbed the kids and we all piled into our jeep and sped away.

"Magnificent spruce trees cover Afognak Island. On high ground, they block the view of the beach so I didn't see the tsunami rush in. But I heard it. The giant wave sounded like any other large wave crashing as it approached the shore, but this one was much louder and it kept coming and coming. We spent that night huddled in the jeep while three separate tsunamis pounded our island.

"The next day we returned home. The waves had reached the level of our windowsills and had pushed the house slightly off the foundation. The rubber seals around the door jambs had held so tightly that only a little water had penetrated the house. We were among the lucky ones on the island. About 25 families lost their homes and all their possessions.

The Nelson family escaped in their jeep and returned to find that their home on Afognak Island had withstood the battering waves of the tsunami.

"The earthquake caused the elevation of Afognak's coastline to sink 5 or 6 feet (1.5– 1.8 m). Salt water flooded the freshwater wells, contaminating our drinking water. And high tides now reached much farther inland than before. We knew that eventually powerful storm waves would sweep away the remaining houses. So the residents decided to relocate the whole village. We chose Port Lions, an undeveloped area on Kodiak Island.

"All of the men in the community came together and helped one another put up the exterior of the new houses. By December, only ten months after the quake, all forty-eight families from Afognak had moved into their new homes."[3]

Alaska is earthquake country and its residents have come to expect minor quakes. The fact that the Good Friday Earthquake occurred did not catch Alaskans by surprise but its intensity did. Never before had they experienced such a powerful temblor.

The Good Friday Earthquake killed 131 people in Alaska. Tsunamis traveling down the West Coast drowned four children in Oregon and a dozen people in Crescent City, California. The tsunamis even sent people scurrying for higher ground in Hawaii. Tsunamis are a recurring problem along the Pacific Ocean coastline. Catastrophic ones can drown thousands of people at one time.

Tsunamis

In 1883 a volcano on the Indonesian island of Krakatau blew apart in one of the most powerful eruptions in history. The explosion pulverized two-thirds of the island and skyrocketed a blast cloud 25 miles (40 km) up into the atmosphere. It also generated an immensely powerful tsunami.

The wave rushed outward from Krakatau in a huge, widening circle. As it approached the neighboring islands of Java and Sumatra, the wave rose higher and higher. By the time it slammed ashore, the tsunami was a mountain of water more than 115 feet (35 m) high, the height of a nine-story building. The wave roared over 165 coastal villages. More gargantuan sea waves followed. About 36,000 people drowned.

Incredibly, landslides can produce even taller tsunamis. In 1958 a tremendous rock-slide plunged into Lituya Bay in Alaska. It generated a wave 1,740 feet (527 m) high that

The dock worker standing on the Commercial Pier in Hilo, Hawaii (foreground left) is about to be overwhelmed by the third and largest wave of the April Fool's Day Tsunami in 1946.

slammed into a hillside on the opposite side of the bay. The wave was higher than three Washington Monuments stacked one on top of another.

In Hawaii, geologists have found signs of prehistoric landslides that produced tsunamis nearly as high. Some sea cliffs on the Hawaiian Islands show scars caused by wave erosion at elevations of nearly 1,200 feet (364 m) above sea level. And there are limestone deposits on cliffs more than 1,000 feet (303 m) above the ocean. The limestone consists of the skeletons of coral and other reef-building organisms found only in shallow ocean water. Geologists believe that a gigantic tsunami ripped the limestone deposits from the ocean floor near shore and deposited them high on the cliffs as it swept over the land.

Most tsunamis are nowhere as large, nor are they triggered by volcanoes or landslides. They are associated with earthquakes beneath the ocean floor, and they pose a great danger. For these are the tsunamis that can zip across deep ocean water virtually undetected and form an immense wall of water as they approach distant shores.

On April 1, 1946, a tsunami spawned by an earthquake in Alaska's Aleutian Islands raced across the Pacific Ocean unnoticed and slammed into the Hawaiian Islands five hours later. Despite traveling more than 2,500 miles (4,000 km), the tsunami retained enough energy to create waves 20 to 32 feet (6 to 10 m) high in Hilo Bay on the Big Island of Hawaii. The first wave struck the Big Island with no warning shortly before 7:00 AM and demolished Hilo's waterfront.

In 1946 Leonie Kawaihona Poy was 15 years old and a student at Laupahoehoe School, located on a peninsula northwest of Hilo Bay. She lived with her father and brother Wilfred in a house that was about 200 hundred feet (61 m) from the school. More than 50 years later the memory of the tsunami was still fresh in her mind:

"On the morning of April 1, I was the first of my family to wake up and I noticed something unusual. When the first school bus arrived at the school, the kids headed straight for the boat landing at the beach. Usually, they stayed near the school building. So I woke up my 11-year-old brother, Wilfred. He rode me on his bicycle down to the landing.

"There wasn't any water on the ocean floor, and the seashore was lined with the many kids who had gotten off the bus. They were all wondering what was going on. I had never heard of tsunamis but I had a gut feeling that something was wrong. So I told my brother that we needed to get home right away and tell our father what the ocean looked like.

Fifteen-year-old Leonie Kawaihona Poy escaped to higher ground with her father and brother, but many of her classmates and neighbors drowned in the tsunami.

"My father was a teacher at the Laupahoehoe School, and a very experienced fisherman. The sea was part of his life. When we got home, we woke him and reported what we had seen. I told him that something must be wrong and that we better leave.

"My father pulled on his clothes and grabbed the keys to our Plymouth. We piled in the car and sped uphill, away from the ocean. I turned to look back and saw the wave coming. It was very high and came over the coconut trees. The kids who had been down by the beach were now running up the road and through the expanse of grass that stretched between the beach and the school. Although I didn't know what was happening, I began to cry because I just knew it was bad. We followed the road farther up the hillside and parked in front of a Japanese church. From there we ran up the road to the stone walls lining it. We sat on the wall and watched.

"We could see the students bobbing in the water but were powerless to save them. Many of our friends and neighbors who had escaped the wave joined us on the wall. One of them was my dear friend, Josephine Lacuesta. We just hugged each other and cried for those we couldn't help. We knew that Josephine's brother Anthony was one of the children who had been swept away by the wave. Twenty-four people from Laupahoehoe drowned that day, most of them children. If my brother's and my curiosity had gotten the best of us, or if my father had wanted to see the ocean floor instead of listening to my plea to flee, we would have been among the dead."[1]

Two people who were caught up in the big wave were Richard Miyashiro and his wife Evelyn. The Miyashiros lived in Waiakea Town, a working-class district with many small shops across the river from Hilo. Their parents were immigrants from Okinawa, Japan, who had come to Hawaii to work in the sugar plantations. Both Evelyn and Richard had been forced to leave school after eighth grade so they

Frantic men who had been working along Hilo's waterfront attempt to outrun the oncoming wave, which is clearly visible in the background. The tsunami killed 159 people in the Hawaiian Islands.

could help support their families. During World War II, Richard served in the U.S. Army with the 100th Battalion in Italy, and was awarded a Purple Heart. When he returned to Hawaii, he and Evelyn opened a small restaurant in Waiakea and named it Café 100, after Richard's unit. The couple made their home above the café.

Evelyn Miyashiro remembered that she and her husband were asleep when the April Fool's Day tsunami struck: "On the morning of April 1, 1946, my husband and I were awakened by the sound of the first tsunami. We fled our home and headed for higher ground—the Wailoa River Bridge. We were alone on the bridge. The first wave had swept safely beneath the bridge and we watched as the second giant wave came in. This wave also went beneath the bridge. But the third surged over the top. My husband and I survived by clinging to the bridge's concrete pillars.

"After the wave ebbed, we fled to higher ground, away from the river. I was five months pregnant with my first child and my progress was slow. So a stevedore [dock worker] carried me to safety. My husband and I had opened our café only three months earlier. Although the tsunami had destroyed it, we decided to rebuild."[2]

After the tragic loss of life in the 1946 tsunami, scientists devised a tsunami warning system. A tsunami *watch* is issued when a 6.75-magnitude or larger earthquake occurs along the Pacific Rim, the land that rings the Pacific Ocean. Then water heights are closely monitored at tidal stations around the Pacific. A tsunami *warning* is declared if the tidal station data shows unusual changes in the sea. Most coastal communities along the west coast of North America, as well as those in Hawaii, have a community warning siren or other signal to alert residents of tsunami threats. Unfortunately, the science of predicting tsunamis has not been perfected and many of the warnings turn out to be false alarms. These false alarms can lull people into a false sense of security.

> "I saw a flash of light and heard a huge crashing sound. Then I felt our house move, and water seeped in through the floor."

Despite their brush with death during the 1946 tsunami, Evelyn and Richard Miyashiro ignored a tsunami warning 14 years later. According to their daughter Gloria Miyashiro Kobayashi, "Café 100 had prospered after it was rebuilt, and by 1960 the family had grown to include three daughters— me, age 13; Kay, 10; and Gail, 6. My parents had purchased some land in Waiakea and built a larger restaurant and a new home in the lot behind it. On May 21, 1960, only three weeks after the opening of the new restaurant, a tsunami warning was issued.

"The sirens blew sometime during the daylight hours. But my family stayed at home, partly because flooding during the 1946 tsunami had not been too severe in this location, and partly because there had been a tsunami warning the week before. We had evacuated then but no wave came, so we felt this was another false alarm.

"My parents went to the river to monitor the waves, while my sisters and I slept in our own beds. Around 1:00 AM, a few minutes before the tsunami struck, my parents returned home. They rang the doorbell to alert us. My two sisters rushed to the living room, but my bedroom was farther away, so I was alone in my room when the wave hit. I saw a flash of light and heard a huge crashing sound. Then I felt our house move,

The Miyashiro family celebrated the grand opening of a new Café 100 in spring 1960. Three weeks later it was destroyed by a tsunami.

and water seeped in through the floor. I was terrified because I couldn't figure out what was happening. After a brief 'ride' in complete darkness, our house became wedged in some rocks and stopped moving. I called for my parents and sisters and was immensely relieved to learn they were all alive. Hours later, Red Cross volunteers came to our rescue.

"The tsunami had completely destroyed the new restaurant. But, the restaurant had saved our lives because it took the brunt of the waves. Once again my parents started over and rebuilt their business."[3]

◆   ◆   ◆

◆　　◆　　◆

If you live or vacation near the seashore, especially one bordering the Pacific Ocean, find out how tsunami alerts are issued in your area. If you hear a tsunami warning, don't go to the beach to watch. Move to higher ground immediately. Most coastal communities along the Pacific have a designated meeting place, such as a school on high ground, where people can safely wait out the tsunami. Tsunamis arrive as a series of waves. The waves may get bigger as they progress. So you will need to remain on high ground until local officials tell you it is safe to leave.

Tsunami warnings alert communities to tsunamis produced by distant earthquakes. The warnings usually give people enough time to evacuate the shore safely. However, if an earthquake occurs locally, it may generate a tsunami that will strike the coast within minutes. There may not be enough time to issue a tsunami alert before the wave hits.

So if you experience a violent earthquake while at the seashore, or if you notice a rapid rise or fall in the ocean level, get to higher ground immediately. One sure sign that a tsunami will strike is when water along the shore suddenly rushes out to sea, stranding fish and boats on the newly exposed ocean bottom.

In 1980, the people living near Mount St. Helens volcano didn't need to concern themselves about tsunamis. They had a different worry.

In Hawaii, local residents grimly survey the wreckage wrought by the 1960 tsunami.

CHAPTER 4

The Day Mount St. Helens Blew Its Top

Geologists have achieved more success in predicting volcanic eruptions than in predicting earthquakes. The Mount St. Helens volcano is a perfect example.

Mount St. Helens stood majestic and silent among the other mountains in Washington State. Snow and ice crowned its rounded summit. Meadows and forests graced its slopes. Near its peak glistened the clear waters of Spirit Lake. Mount St. Helens attracted hikers, campers, fishing enthusiasts, and lumberjacks. Few of these visitors could imagine that deep within this magnificent mountain a violent volcano brewed. But in 1975 volcanologists had recognized the danger and predicted that Mount St.

The May 18, 1980 eruption of Mount St. Helens reduced the volcano's height from 9,677 feet (2950 m) to 8,367 feet (2550 m).

Helens would erupt within 25 years.

Just five years later, in March 1980, the volcano stirred. Earthquakes rattled Mount St. Helens. Soon steam and ash puffed from a vent at the peak. Volcanologists rushed to study the mountain. Small eruptions continued into April.

Long, steady tremors replaced the sharper earthquake bursts, signaling the upward movement of magma. From the inside, molten rock pressed against the mountaintop. A second vent opened. Gradually the two vents expanded until they joined and formed one huge crater that continued to grow. Worried that a violent eruption was imminent, the volcanologists advised local officials to block off the area within 15 miles (24 km) of the crater. People living within this danger zone were asked to leave. Most complied, even though some did not believe the volcano posed a threat. Roads leading to the summit were off limits to residents and sightseers.

By late April the north face began to bulge and crack. The bulge grew quickly. By mid-May it was 1 mile (1.6 km) long, more than ½ mile (0.8 km) wide, and protruded nearly 500 feet (150 m) from the original mountain surface.

In the spring of 1980 Keith Ronnholm was a graduate student studying geophysics at the University of Washington in Seattle. His sense of adventure led him to do something that was extremely unsafe: He went for a close look at Mount St. Helens and was lucky to escape with his life.

> "The thought of a volcano erupting almost in my own backyard excited me."

Ronnholm recalled, "The thought of a volcano erupting almost in my own backyard excited me. One Saturday in mid-May, I decided to view the volcano up close. At the time, small eruptions of ash and steam were occurring about every eight days. I hoped to capture one of these outbursts on film.

"To prevent tourists from venturing too close to the volcano, the National Guard had set up roadblocks on the main roads. So I drove my pickup truck up a steep and winding gravel road built for loggers. I ended up at Bear Meadow, a ridge 10 miles [16 km] northeast of Mount St. Helens. I chose this spot because two ridges lay between it and the crater. I figured that the ridges would act as barriers, protecting me from any pyroclastic flows—clouds of super-hot ash and gas. In addition, Bear Meadow provided a perfect view of the crater.

"I noticed four or five other cars parked nearby—I was not alone in my search for adventure. For the rest of the day I watched the mountain, waiting for something to happen. But nothing did. That night I slept in the back of my truck.

"The next morning I awoke at 5:30 AM and admired the beauty of the mountain as it reflected the golden red glow of the sunrise. Since there wasn't even a puff of steam coming from the crater or any other sign of activity, I went back to sleep. Around 8:00 AM I woke up again and began reading in bed.

"Half an hour later I heard some yelling. I rolled over and saw the entire north face of the mountain sliding downhill. Then a puff of dark gray ash began to billow out of the area vacated by the landslide. I remember thinking, 'Wow! I'm going to get to see an eruption.'"

Two mountain ridges did little to protect Keith Ronnholm from the enormous, fast-moving ash cloud created by the eruption of Mount St. Helens.

Water was locked within the rock that formed Mount St. Helens. The magma superheated this water to a temperature far beyond the normal boiling point. However, because it was under tremendous pressure with no place to expand, the water remained a liquid. On the morning of May 18, 1980, a large earthquake jarred the mountain. The bulge on the north face started to break loose and slide down the mountain. With the pressure released, the superheated water exploded violently into steam. It shattered the surrounding rock. Unleashed, the steam blasted out sideways through the avalanche, propelling with it ash, rock, and other debris in its path.

At this point Ronnholm grabbed his camera and began clicking the shutter. He recalled: "The landslide continued its downward plunge and the blast cloud billowed out sideways but I didn't hear any noise. Within 30 seconds from the start of the eruption the blast cloud surged over the most distant ridge between the volcano and me. The cloud swirled over the ridge like a big wave crashing over a breakwater. It was headed right for me! I realized the ridges would provide no protection."

Traveling at speeds up to 330 miles (528 km) per hour, this "stone wind" scorched and leveled everything for miles around. It snapped millions of trees at their bases. Meanwhile, the avalanche roared down the mountain. Hot gases from the blast swept over snow and ice fields, melting them instantly. The resulting water mixed with the loose rock and earth from the avalanche to form boiling walls of surging mud.

As the eruption cloud headed toward Ronnholm, he threw on his clothes and snapped another picture. Ronnholm said: "I remember finding only one sock and thinking it probably didn't matter if I left the other one behind. By the time I got the truck started and turned around, the cloud had swept over the second ridge. It was swooping toward the valley in front of me."

The force of the initial sideways blast fractured the rock capping the mountaintop, prompting a second explosion. This one headed upward. An enormous plume of hot rock and ash zoomed 12 miles (19 km) high and formed a dark cloud that filled the sky. Rocks and ash pelted the countryside below. At first, mostly old rocks were hurled from the crater. Later ash and pumice from fresh magma streamed out.

The dark cloud rapidly expanded and drifted to the northeast, spreading rock, pumice, and ash over the entire area. The eruption of Mount St. Helens killed 57 people.

Ronnholm snapped pictures as he sped away. He recollected, "I raced down the logging road at 40 miles [64 km] an hour—twice as fast as the steep windy road was meant to be driven.... A wall of gray ash rose...into the air behind me. Lightning bolts bounced from one part of the cloud to another.... Gradually, it drifted over my head, filling more and more of the sky.

"Strange noises came from the forest. Then a golf-ball-sized rock slammed into the dirt 20 feet [6 m] away from me and made a crater. It dawned on me that the noise came

The standing dead zone was the outermost fringe of the blast area. Here the blast was still hot enough to kill trees but not strong enough to knock them down.

from rocks striking the trees. The rocks had been part of Mount St. Helens's summit. . . . As I drove away, rocks bounced off of my truck like hailstones. . . . Within a minute drops of mud . . . replaced the rocks and splattered the windshield. . . . Soon dry ash replaced the mud.

"The sky darkened and I slowed the truck to 5 miles [8 km] an hour because I could barely see the road. Ash began to seep into the vehicle even though the windows and vents were closed. I moistened a handkerchief and breathed through it. Then the sky turned pitch-black and I could no longer find my way. The logging road wound around a steep mountainside. It lacked guardrails and in places the side of the road dropped 50 to 100 feet [15 to 30 m]. To avoid plunging over a cliff, I turned off the engine and sat in the dark. . . .

"Ten minutes went by . . . and then in the rearview mirror I noticed a red glow. . . . A logging truck pulled alongside me. Two loggers walked in front of it, guiding the driver. Three or four cars followed the truck and I pulled in line behind them. Traveling bumper to bumper we made our way down the mountain. . . ."[1]

The volcano erupted for nine hours. Prevailing winds carried the ash northeastward. Blizzardlike, it fell from the sky, covering eastern Washington and parts of Montana and Idaho with a gray coating that resembled dirty snow.

Like Keith Ronnholm, Mike Moore had originally come for a close look at Mount St.

Helens, only Moore brought along his wife Lu, and their daughters Bonnie Lu, age 4, and Terra, 3 months. Luckily, they changed their plans and decided to camp on the Green River Valley on Mount St. Helens's flank. Thirteen miles (21 km), several 6,000-foot (1,800 m) peaks and a 5,000-foot (1,500 m) ridge separated the family from the site of the eruption. But that wasn't enough. With the onset of the eruption Mike and Lu were plunged into a struggle they are unlikely to forget, a struggle to save their own lives and the lives of their children.

Moore provided a detailed description of their adventure in an unpublished account: "As the eruption cloud descended upon us, we decided our best chance of survival would be to take shelter in a dilapidated hunter's shack nearby. Before our eyes, the ash turned the lush valley into a lifeless gray moonscape. The ashfall increased rapidly and completely blotted out the sun.

"For about 30 minutes we were plunged into total darkness. It was like being in a deep cave with no light source. We soaked some socks in water and placed them across our noses and mouths so we could breathe without inhaling ash. During this we had covered Baby Terra under blankets and a plastic tarp. She never cried or made any other sounds. So Lu pinched her to make sure she was alive.

"Thunder boomed all around us with an almost earsplitting intensity. Even more ominous were the tremendous explosions coming from the mountain. Although we never heard the initial blast, it now sounded as if the mountain were blowing itself apart. The noises scared Bonnie Lu. When we told her what was happening, she decided the ash was the devil's snow. Giving it a name made her feel better.

"...it now sounded as if the mountain were blowing itself apart."

"A few hours after the eruption the ash cloud lightened up enough that we decided to hike back to our car. We thought the trek would take about two hours because the trail was fairly level and the distance was only 2½ miles [4 km].

"The trail was remarkably easy to find at first. The smooth ash coating made it look like a concrete sidewalk. About 1 mile [1.6 km] from camp we crossed our first downed tree, one we had crossed on the way in. However, then we came to an area with newly fallen trees and some standing ones.

"The fallen trees blocked the trail and we had to go around them. We brushed against small trees and bushes, sending ash into the air. With every step, ash fell on us or blew into our eyes. So much ash had gotten into my eyes that I could not see and

Mike Moore and his daughter, 3-year-old Bonnie Lu, survived the blast. Bonnie Lu called the falling ash "the devil's snow."

A paramedic (left) was amazed to find Lu Moore (right) and her family alive the day after the eruption.

my eyes hurt terribly. Fear overwhelmed me but Lu rinsed my eyes out and within 15 minutes we were able to resume our escape attempt.

"About 1 mile [1.6 km] from our car the trail ended abruptly. In front of us lay an area of utter destruction. All the trees had been blown down. Some of them were 4 feet [1.2 m] thick and were perched on top of other downed logs. We could not skirt the area because it was too vast and the surrounding mountain slopes too steep.

"We were too exhausted to go any farther, so we decided to pitch our tent and rest for the night. With the coming of morning our spirits rose. By 10:00 AM we were ready to set out again. Suddenly we heard the sound of an approaching helicopter. Lu and Bonnie both wore bright red coats and within a few minutes the helicopter pilot had spotted us. The first copter was soon joined by a second and they dropped a paramedic to the ground. The paramedic couldn't believe we were alive and he was even more amazed when he learned that one of us was only 3 months old." [2]

During the next five months Mount St. Helens erupted five more times, but the eruptions were much smaller than the May 18 blast. In October 1980 a lava dome began to grow in the crater. (A lava dome is a rounded pile of thick lava. It expands when magma oozes in beneath it during an eruption and inflates the dome like a water balloon. When the lava breaks through the dome's hardened outer crust, it slowly spills over the sides, widening the dome farther.) For six years, small occasional eruptions increased the size of the dome and then they petered out.

Although Mount St. Helens has quieted substantially since 1980, it has not gone back to sleep. Scientists continue to monitor the volcano closely for signs of activity.

PART 2

Monster Storms

Could anything be more frightening than being caught up in a power-ful earthquake, swept away by a tsunami, or witnessing a volcano explode? Survivors of lethal tornadoes, hurricanes, and blizzards may think they have experienced the ultimate fright. Monster storms can create as much havoc as volcanoes and earthquakes, and inspire just as much fear.

Like volcanoes and earthquakes, monster storms are powered by heat. However, their heat source does not arise from inside Earth. It comes from an external source—the sun. As the sun shines on Earth, it heats the land and water. In turn, the land and water heat the air molecules close above them. But the sun does not heat Earth's surface evenly. Some places receive more solar energy than others. This unequal heating leads to uneven pressure pat-terns, which create winds in the atmosphere, the immense ocean of air cloaking our planet. These winds can range in strength from gentle breezes to tornado-force winds.

The equator receives far more of the sun's energy than the north and south poles. So the air above the equator is much warmer than the air above the polar regions. Warm air expands, rises, and is lighter than cold air. And it doesn't exert as much pressure as cold air does. As a result warm air creates lows—vast areas of low pressure in the atmosphere. Lows are the key ingredient in the formation of tornadoes, hurricanes, and blizzards.

When a mass of cold, heavy, high-pressure air from the polar regions—a high—drifts toward the equator, it collides with a low from this tropical region. The air masses do not mix smoothly. Instead they clash along their edges, creating stormy weather. Winds increase when cool air drops down to take the place of rising warm air. The greater the pressure difference between the high and the low, the faster the wind blows. If the pressure difference is great enough, a tornado or blizzard may form, depending on other conditions of the atmosphere. A hurricane low doesn't require the presence of a nearby high. It just needs plenty of warm, humid, tropical air.

Tornadoes are whirling, funnel-shaped clouds that dip down from thunderheads. They have their beginnings in the thin line of thunderstorms that form where air masses clash. In the central United States, April, May, and June are prime months for the formation of tornadoes. Under the right conditions, winds in a thundercloud rotate around a center of low pressure at tremendous speeds, creating a funnel. The strongest tornadoes may have wind speeds that exceed 300 miles (480 km) per hour. That is 100 miles (160 km) per hour more than the winds of the mightiest hurricanes. The storms that produce tornadoes may last for hours, but the life span of each individual tornado is usually measured in minutes.

Unlike tornadoes, which can form over land or water, hurricanes develop over ocean waters near the equator in late summer and early fall. The surface temperature of tropical oceans climbs to 79°F (26°C) or higher. An immense amount of water evaporates from the warm oceans and goes into the air as water vapor. When this warm moist air rises, it collides with cooler, dryer air above it. The collision often triggers violent thunderstorms, which sometimes form clusters and grow into organized lows. About ten percent of these thunderstorms develop into hurricanes.

A spiral wall of clouds forms around the center of low pressure—the *eye* of the storm. Within the clouds, winds scream, rains pelt down, and thunderbolts slash the air. A hurricane is born. It careens over the water like a rapidly spinning top, advancing at a rate of 10 to 30 miles (16 to 48 km) per hour.

Hurricanes can vary from 300 to 1,000 (480 to 1600 km) miles in diameter, but the eyes range from 3 to 40 miles (5 to 64 km) across. The eye is a calm, low-pressure area, often with a cloudless sky above it. But the winds in the clouds around the eye are the most violent of the hurricane, with a minimum speed of 74 miles (118 km) per hour. In the most powerful hurricanes the winds may reach 200 miles (320 km) per hour. Hurricanes with wind speeds exceeding 150 miles (240 km) per hour rarely occur. Because hurricanes are so large and they advance so slowly, their strong winds have much time to cause considerable damage as they pass over the communities in their path.

Hurricane winds can topple trees and collapse buildings, and the torrential rains can produce massive flooding. However, the waves generated by the hurricane are the most destructive force of the storm. As a hurricane moves toward land it kicks up waves 10 to 15 feet (3 to 4.5 m) higher than normal, inflicting considerable damage to the coastline. Near the eye of the hurricane, the low air pressure and strong winds lift the surface of the ocean into a rolling mound. As the mound moves ashore, the ocean floor slows its movement and pushes it higher. This creates a storm surge, a rapidly rising tide that may raise the level of the ocean 15 feet (4.5 m) or higher. Huge, wind-whipped waves arrive atop the storm surge and batter everything in their path.

Blizzards are sometimes called "white hurricanes." They are severe winter storms characterized by heavy snowfall, frigid temperatures, and strong winds. Like true hurricanes, blizzards can churn up waves, giving coastlines a fierce pounding. In the open ocean both hurricanes and blizzards can build up waves to tremendous heights. In 1978, thirty-foot-high (9 m) waves generated by a monster blizzard sunk a 45-foot (14 m) pilot boat off the New England coast. But 78 years earlier, an even more ferocious storm was responsible for the destruction of an entire city.

CHAPTER 5

The 1900 Galveston Hurricane

The worst natural disaster in U.S. history—the Galveston Hurricane—was a catastrophe waiting to happen. In 1900 Galveston was the fourth largest city in Texas, with a population of 38,000. The municipality sat atop a barrier island in the Gulf of Mexico. The island measured 25 miles (40 km) long, 2 miles (3 km) wide, and in most places, a mere 5 feet (1.5 m) above sea level. Four bridges connected Galveston to the mainland, 2 miles (3 km) away.

On September 4, 1900, Galveston residents paid little heed to weather reports concerning a tropical storm disturbance moving northward over Cuba. Tropical storms

---

Despite efforts of Galveston residents to build houses to withstand Gulf storms, the structures were no match for the fury of the 1900 hurricane.

were common in the late fall. The citizens of Galveston had adapted to "overflows," occasional storm-driven floods. They had constructed the first floors of their homes and businesses several feet (1 m) above the ground. Overflows were often regarded as an excuse for an unplanned holiday, in the same way major snowstorms are viewed in the northern parts of the United States.

By Friday morning, September 7, the tropical storm had pounded Cuba, rolled over the tip of Florida, and then unexpectedly veered due west across the Gulf of Mexico. Weathermen Isaac Cline, the chief of the U.S. Weather Bureau's Galveston office, and his brother Joseph, the bureau's chief clerk, became increasingly alarmed. The storm seemed destined to strike Galveston.

Isaac hoisted two warning flags on a pole atop the building where their office was located. Most of Galveston's citizens could interpret the flags. The first meant that a storm of marked violence was expected. The other indicated the direction of the storm's approach.

Worried about the weather, Joseph Cline slept poorly that night. He later wrote in his memoirs: "About four o'clock in the morning, I awoke, filled with a sense of impending disaster...I sensed that the waters of the Gulf were already over our back yard. One glance out of the south window facing the Gulf showed me that my presentiment was correct. I immediately awoke my brother [and we] decided upon our division of labor. I was to [return to the weather office]. He was to remain on the beach, warning people....."[1]

> "About four o'clock in the morning, I awoke, filled with a sense of impending disaster..."

Isaac Cline had the more difficult task of the two brothers. In his autobiography he described his experience: "I harnessed my horse to a two wheeled cart...and drove along the beach from one end of town to the other. I warned the people that great danger threatened them, and advised some 6,000 persons from the interior of the State, who were summering along the beach to go home immediately. I warned persons residing within three blocks of the beach to move to the higher portions of the city."[2]

While a large number of people followed Isaac's advice, others thronged to the shore from other parts of the island to admire nature's spectacle. Many of these spectators remained unconcerned even when gigantic waves destroyed the piers and a bathhouse.

A gentle rain began to fall around 8:45 AM. Throughout the morning the winds steadily picked up speed, the rain began to pour down, and the tide rose rapidly, flooding low-lying areas. By noon the situation was clearly becoming dangerous. Many families living along the beachfront abandoned their houses and sought shelter in buildings in more elevated portions of the island.

By midafternoon the rain was whipping in nearly horizontal sheets and the wind was blowing so hard it could knock a person down. Wildly churning, the sea now covered half the city, and swept away the bridges to the mainland. Escape from the island was impossible, and it was even too late for people to safely seek higher ground on the island itself. The Cline brothers realized there was little more they could do in their official capacity.

Isaac Cline, chief of the U. S. Weather Bureau's Galveston office, drove a horse-drawn carriage miles along the beach to warn residents and vacationers about the impending storm.

The only thing left for Isaac Cline to do was to alert his superiors: "I recognized at 3:30 p.m. that an awful disaster was upon us. I wrote a message to send to the Chief of the Weather Bureau at Washington, advising him of the terrible situation, and stated that the city was fast going under water, that great loss of life must result, and stressed the need for relief....There remained nothing else I could do to help the people.... I waded nearly two miles [3 km] to my home through water, often above my waist. Hurricane winds were driving timbers and slates through the air every where around me...."[3]

By 5:15 PM the wind speeds reached 100 miles (160 km) per hour and the raging water covered the entire island. The highest sections were submerged in 4 to 5 feet (1.2 to 1.5 m) of water, and the low-lying areas in more than 10 feet (3 m). The fierce winds wrenched roofs from houses and hurtled debris through the sky. As buildings buckled, terrified men, women, and children were buried in the falling debris or catapulted into the water. Not even the dead entombed in the island's cemeteries were safe from the storm's fury. The thundering surf unearthed their coffins and tossed them around in the waves.

Isaac Cline had designed his home with hurricanes in mind. Nearly 50 people had taken refuge in it, including Isaac; his pregnant wife; three daughters, ages 6, 11, and 12; and his brother Joseph. About 6:30 PM the water abruptly rose 4 more feet (1.2 m) and slammed down on the island. Many houses that had withstood the previous onslaught collapsed, sending more wreckage into the wild tide. Within an hour the water rose yet another 5 feet (1.5 m), and Cline's house was the only one left standing in his neighborhood.

But even Isaac Cline's sturdy house was being severely battered by the hurricane. He recalled: "The rapid rise in the storm tide soon forced us to the second story. Here we could see wreckage being tossed by the winds and waves, driven against buildings and breaking [the buildings] to pieces, thus increasing the wreckage for the waves to use as battering rams as they rushed forward....We probably would have weathered the storm, but a trestle, about one fourth of a mile [0.4 km] long...was carried squarely against the side of the house... the house creaked and was carried over into the surging waters...." [4]

Joseph Cline described what happened as the house plunged into the storm-tossed sea: "I had taken my position near a window on the windward side, and, as the house capsized, I seized the hand of each of my brother's two [older] children, turned my back toward the window, and...smashed through the glass and the wooden storm shutters, still gripping the hands of the two youngsters. The momentum hurled us all through the window as the [house tipped over].

"The two youngsters and I were alone on the top side....All the other occupants of that room, nearly fifty men, women, and children, it appeared were still trapped inside, for the house had not yet broken up....There was no means of egress except the window through which I had smashed my way clear....The children were clinging to me for protection from the wind and flying debris. I put them gently aside for a moment and lowered the top part of my body between the casing of the window which I had broken. I cupped my mouth with my hands and called into the room as loudly as possible: 'Come here! Come here!' No answer came from the black depth beneath me. I had heard that the drowning would seize and cling to any object within reach. I lowered my legs through the window frame, letting them swing back and forth and around in the water.... I had hoped that some of the trapped ones within the room might catch my feet and so be pulled out. My efforts were wasted and I finally gave them up. I have no words to tell the agony of heart I experienced in that moment.

"Little by little the house had been breaking up. In spite of the added danger that lay in this development, my heart suddenly leaped with uncontrollable joy. In two figures that clung to the drift about one hundred feet [30 m] to leeward, I discovered my brother and his youngest child."[5]

Isaac Cline described his miraculous escape: "I with my wife and baby, six years old, were in the center of the room. We were thrown by the impact into a triple chimney and were carried down under the wreckage to the bottom of the water. My wife's clothing was entangled in the wreckage and she never rose from the water. I was pinned under the timbers and thought I would be drowned. The last thought that I remembered that passed through my mind was this—'I have done all that could have been done in this disaster, the world will know that I did my duty to the last, it is useless to fight for life. I will let the water enter my lungs and pass on.' However, it was not my time to go. When I regained consciousness, I was floating with my body hanging between heavy timbers which had pressed the water out of my lungs. A flash of lightning revealed my baby girl floating on wreckage a few feet [1 m] away. I struggled out of the timbers and reached her. A few minutes later during another flash I saw my brother and my other two children clinging to the wreckage. I took my baby and joined them on the floating debris. . . .

"In order to avoid being killed by flying timbers, we placed the children in front of us, turned our backs to the winds and held planks . . . to our backs to distribute and lighten the blows which the wind driven debris was showering upon us continually. . . ."[6]

At one point it seemed that all would be lost. According to Joseph: "A weather-battered hulk that had once been a house came bearing down upon us. . . .The huge derelict was sweeping beneath it everything that lay in its path. I was conscious of being direly frightened but I retained sufficient presence of mind to leap as the monster reached us and to get a grip with my hands on the highest edge of the wreck. My weight was enough to drag it perceptibly lower in the water, and I called to my brother,

> "I have done all that could have been done in this disaster, the world will know that I did my duty to the last..."

who added his weight to my own. Together we were able to pull the upper side downward and we climbed thankfully on the top with the children, just as the drift upon which we had been floating went to pieces under our feet....

"For three hours, from eight to eleven, we floated on a multitude of drifts, by turns. We were swept out to sea for such a distance that finally we could see no lights anywhere. Suddenly, however, the wind [shifted] and our courses turned landward again. We finally floated back— sufficiently close to shore for the light to reappear....

"...two other castaways, a man and a woman, joined us on the wreckage that, at that time,

Galveston residents seeking refuge from the hurricane filled the Sacred Heart Church (above left), but their sanctuary turned into a deathtrap. The number of people who perished here is unknown.

was serving us as a lifeboat. The strangers remained with us for some little time until the man crawled up to where I sat, pulled the two children away, and tried to shelter himself behind my body. I pushed him indignantly away and drew the children back. He repeated the unspeakable performance. This time I drew out a knife that I carried, and threatened him with it. I warned him that I would use it on him if he attempted such an action again....

"We had to keep moving from one insecure float to another, as each went to pieces. By now we had floated back into the southern edge of the city, and for the first time could hear cries for help. The calls were coming from a large two-story house standing directly in the path of the drifting mass which we had made our latest refuge.... Next moment our mass struck the house, demolishing it and no doubt scattering the inhabitants into the water and darkness.

"My brother was struck and knocked down by one of the hurtling timbers, and all

By Sunday morning the water receded. Dazed survivors left their shelters to take stock of their losses.

my attention was directed to him. I found, to my relief, that he was not badly hurt. After he was on his feet again, I noticed a little girl struggling in the water. Under the impression that she was my brother's youngest child, I managed to catch her garments before she floated out of reach. I set her upon the drift with the rest of us. She was smaller than the other two, and, still believing she was my niece who had been washed overboard when her father was hurt, I placed her beside me for greater safety. . . .

"Our drift began to open into holes, which often closed quickly again as the timbers worked back and forth. The oldest child fell into one of these, and I had barely caught her up from the watery void before it closed again. I thrust her back into safety, but she called to her father in a panic, 'Papa! Papa! Uncle Joe is neglecting Rosemary and me for this strange child!' For the first time I looked closely at the little girl I had fished out of the water some time before. I then glanced over my shoulder at my

More than 6,000 people died as a result of the storm. Four to ten feet (1.2 to 3 m) of debris extended for miles.

brother. He was still bending protectively over his baby. The child I had rescued, therefore, was not my niece but a stranger. I kept her with the other two at my side until we reached the point from which a light was shining. It was a house and it was on solid ground.

"In that building, surrounded by wreckage, we made our landing about one hour before midnight. Tired and unspeakably battered, we climbed through an upstairs window into a room from which the roof and ceiling had been blown away. Just under the floor of the room, the black waters of the Gulf were lapping.... At any rate, we had something solid beneath our feet again, and in that room we thankfully rested the remainder of that Saturday night."[7]

By 2:00 AM Sunday morning the storm was over and the floodwaters had begun to recede. By dawn, the water had subsided from the streets. The stunned survivors found the entire island littered with rubble and corpses. Some 6,000 people had died.

Joseph Cline described the scene that unfolded before them as they left their refuge: "As we emerged [from the house] dreadful sights met our gaze on all sides. From the time we descended the stairs to make our way to the home of some acquaintances in the city's center, we climbed over dead bodies sprawled and piled where the flood had left them, and over heaps of wreckage. Debris from four to ten feet [1.2 to 3 m] deep and extending for blocks packed with dead was all that was left of thousands of homes and the human beings who had lived in them just one day earlier.... The inevitable looting had already begun. We had made our way only four blocks when we observed pilferers at work on bodies and possessions.... I even came upon some thieves breaking into my own trunk, which had washed far from what had been my home.

"The strange child that I had lifted out of the drift proved to be the seven-year-old daughter of parents whose home was in San Antonio.... I left her in charge of the people living in the house wherein we had 'landed'.... I left her weeping bitterly at being parted from her new-found friend, but safe and in good hands.

"Some days later, still shaken and ill from the experience of that dreadful night, I entered a drugstore to buy some medicine. A grief-stricken man stood at the counter in earnest conversation with the druggist. I overheard him say he was living in San Antonio. Acting upon a sudden impulse, I drew nearer and asked him if he knew a little girl called Cora Goldbeck.

"I shall never forget his face, lined with dread and horror, as he replied, 'She is my daughter.'

"'Then your daughter is safe,' I told him."[8]

Within four years after the hurricane, Galveston had constructed a 17-foot-high (5 m) seawall that surrounded the city like a fortress. It took another six years to pump enough sand behind the seawall to raise the elevation of the city. The effort paid off in 1915 when a hurricane with the force of the one in 1900 slammed into the island. This time fewer than a dozen people died. The citizens of Galveston had clearly demonstrated that emergency preparedness saves lives. It is unlikely that the city will ever be caught unprepared for a hurricane again. Sadly, however, this was not the case for the people of Providence, Rhode Island, in 1938.

CHAPTER 6

The New England Hurricane of 1938

New England is not known as hurricane country. So no one took much notice on Tuesday, September 20, 1938, when a hurricane in the Atlantic Ocean barreled northward, nearly parallel to the U.S. coastline. Weather forecasters predicted that the storm would veer out to sea before it reached Cape Hatteras, North Carolina. In the Northeast, weather reports called for cloudy skies with the possibility of heavy rains the next day.

On Wednesday morning, residents along the coasts of New York and southern New England noticed that the weather was "queerly warm" and the waves unusually large.

Debris from hundreds of shattered coastal homes washed up on shore at Sandy Hill Cove, Rhode Island, after the hurricane. Communities from Long Island to Maine were devastated by the monster storm.

Instead of blowing out to sea, the hurricane had picked up speed and continued northward. Lacking the storm-tracking technology it has today, the National Weather Service lost sight of the storm's path until it was too late to issue an adequate warning.

Edith Anderson, age 38, was at her job in Providence, Rhode Island, when she realized a bad storm was heading her way: "As the pace of the winds began to get worse and the momentum of the storm seemed to be quickening, I received a call from Elsie [the woman she carpooled with]. She asked if I could make it to the parking lot. She wanted to get a head start and beat the storm home.

"Against the advice of my boss and co-workers, I left. . . . I had gotten as far as Eddy Street down by the Court House and the wind had grown progressively worse in a matter of minutes. I had stopped for just a moment when some kind of tin sign blew from out of nowhere and grazed me. I was extremely frightened now, and very concerned for my safety. . . .

"I felt, for the first time, that I was going to be killed. The tremendous winds seemed to be gaining power with every second. It took all of my strength just to stand. . . . The walk on a normal day would have taken me no more than ten minutes. I had lost track of time and it seemed, because of my frequent stops to grab onto something and to gain my bearings, the journey lasted well over an hour. . . .

"Great sheets of rain had started to come down before I reached [my destination], the Grosvenor Building. When Elsie saw me she said that she had never seen such a sight in all her life. I had a hat plastered to my head. . . . My hair was a mess and sticking out in every direction and my clothes were ruined. Elsie said a drowned rat would have looked more presentable at that moment. I stood before Elsie and her co-workers thankful just to be alive."[1]

> "The tremendous winds seemed to be gaining power with every second."

Atop the Empire State Building in New York City, wind instruments measured gusts of 120 miles (192 km) per hour. Rain pounded down in nearly horizontal sheets. Subways and roads flooded. But the city did not receive the full brunt of the hurricane's fury.

To the east, the eye of the hurricane sped toward Long Island. The raging wind and torrential rains arrived first. Around 4:00 PM came the storm surge. Initially, it appeared to onlookers to be a thick fog rolling in from the ocean. As it approached the shore,

The storm surge swamped these cars parked in the business district in downtown Providence, Rhode Island.

however, the terrified spectators realized it was a 30-foot (9 m) wall of water. The wall of water thundered across the low-lying beach communities, leveling homes and snuffing out lives.

The hurricane then battered southern New England. At Misquamicut Beach, a Rhode Island vacation hamlet, the storm surge struck again without warning. One minute vacationers were bracing doors and windows to protect their houses against wind and rain. The next minute a wall of water engulfed them. Forty-one people perished. But Misquamicut was not unique. All of Rhode Island's coastal communities suffered similar fates.

The state's capital, Providence, located 30 miles (48 km) from the open sea at the top of Narragansett Bay, suffered the worst of the storm surge. As the bay narrowed, the wall of water rose higher and higher. It roared ashore with incredible intensity,

After the hurricane, waterlogged cars and a tangle of debris clogged the piers of Providence's waterfront. The storm surge drove an excursion boat into the wharf.

splintering wharves, plucking boats from moorings, and crushing houses. Streets in the business district were covered by as much as 13¾ feet (4.2 m) of water.

Edith Anderson recalled the sight: "We looked out Elsie's office window and could see a parking area [by the river]. The water had [risen] throughout the storm and was climbing up the sides of the cars. We could see the headlights coming on and [hear] the cacophonous sounds of horns blowing as the [salt water] caused electrical systems to short circuit." [2]

On the Connecticut shore, high seas nearly swept away the *Bostonian*, a Boston-bound train with 275 passengers aboard. Harry W. Easton, the train's engineer, had worked for the New York, New Haven and Hartford Railroad for forty years. In that time he had seen many a bad storm, but nothing like the Hurricane of 1938. Several years

Opposite: The storm surge transformed the streets of downtown Providence into rushing waterways, and Providence City Hall into a virtual island.

later Easton wrote about his experience in *Railroad Magazine*:

"When I picked up [the] signal to leave New Haven . . . rain was still crashing down and a hearty wind was rolling papers across the track. Off Branford I caught a view of Long Island Sound, and the violence of the whitecaps took me by surprise. . . .

"One caution signal flashed after another, but these were hardly needed as I was keeping Number 14 well under control. Meanwhile water was creeping insidiously over the tracks. I feared that any minute the rails might start to wobble under us. . . . When we reached [New London] at 3:10 that afternoon, half an hour late, the water around the station was up to the tracks. Big boats were tossing in the harbor like chips, while small craft, capsized, were drifting helplessly out to sea. . . .

"We swished past Mystic at barely twenty miles [32 km] an hour and were soon near the Stonington causeway, a strip of double track laid across an arm of the ocean on boulders [and crushed gravel]. Creeping up on this structure I could see that breakers were hitting the rocks and tumbling across the [rails]. . . .

> "I feared that any minute the rails might start to wobble under us."

"Cutting down to the pace of a slug, I glanced at the water, now boiling over the track. You could feel the train shiver as waves smashed against the car sides. Not a good place to be stopped, I was thinking. The track won't hold out. . . ."

About 600 feet (182 m) from the mainland Easton received the red signal to stop. Reluctantly he brought the train to a halt. He pulled down the whistle cord to alert the signalman and get permission to proceed. But the howling wind masked the shrieks of the whistle and the signalman never heard it. The signal stayed red. So Easton decided to approach the signalman on foot.

Easton recalled: "Down the rungs I climbed into the knee-deep, boiling briny. Surf sprayed and blinded me, soaked me to the skin. . . . For every step I took forward, the wind blew me back a yard [meter]. . . . A storm-driven log cracked me in the knee and threw me down, almost submerged [me], but instinct set me on my feet again. . . . At length I slogged ashore bruised and dripping. . . ."

Easton reached the signal tower and convinced the signalman to permit him to move the train off the causeway. The water was waist-deep by the time he returned to the train and several of the coaches were leaning far over toward the sea. He recalled the conversation he had with the conductor:

"'What are you going to do?' asked [the conductor].

"'Get out of here,' I replied, 'whether there are any tracks or not.'"

Easton then ordered the crew to herd the passengers into the baggage car behind the locomotive and uncouple it from the rest of the cars.

Easton described what happened next: "As the two hundred and seventy-five passengers poured into the aisles, some began to shove; others opened doors and leaped into four feet [1.2 m] of moving water. I saw a Negro porter wading waist-deep with a small child on each shoulder and a woman clinging to his coat tails. He got them safely aboard the baggage car. We did not know it then, but one of the dining-car employees lost his life when he plunged in to save a drowning woman. The name of Chester A. Walker has been added to the long list of railroad heroes....

"Large hunks of debris were whirling in front of the [locomotive]. I pulled back the throttle, but we had barely started when—bang! A booming to the rear was followed by a jolt which rocked the engine and brought us to a dead stop. Some floating colossus had struck the baggage car...and locked the [emergency] brakes....

"Again I shoved the throttle...but the locked brakes held. Angrily I pulled the throttle back as far as it would go. The big modern engine bolted, groaned, and to my great relief slowly moved, dragging the [baggage] car despite its locked wheels.

"A light rowboat drifted into our path; we cracked it like a shell. Something began to drag us. Telegraph wires, thrown down by the storm, were tangled around our boiler. A mass of them held us in their fingers...but they quickly let go as we snapped the pole....

"Just as I thought all might be clear, a large hulk loomed in the darkness ahead....My heart stopped when I saw it was a house which the storm had thrown on our track....We neared the rising and falling structure until our [locomotive] gently touched it. The cab shivered and windows rattled but we kept on pushing....The hulk turned just a little and stopped. Then the gale caught the house and drove it into fast-gliding water, which carried it crazily out to sea.

"Crates, logs and small boats kept smashing against our [locomotive]. Just as I thought the worst might be over,

> "Just as I thought all might be clear, a large hulk loomed in the darkness ahead."

Harry Easton and the passengers aboard the Bostonian *abandoned all but two cars. The empty train cars perched precariously on the Stonington causeway.*

something heavy thumped the front end. A full-sized sailboat, tilted to one side, was lodged on the track....Slowly our wheels ground forward. The boat was firmly wedged. ...My hand could feel the deep vibration as the engine's power drove against the heavy barrier of wood....

"We were stopped now, maybe for the last time. But no; something snapped....The craft revolved sickly, turned bottom up, and began humping rapidly for shore....Roaring her triumph, the big engine nosed ashore....When I looked back I could see sparks streaming from the wheels but I kept right on to the crossing near the [Stonington] station before I stopped and thanked God we were safe...." [3]

From the coasts of Connecticut and Rhode Island, the hurricane ripped northward through the rest of New England before reaching far into Canada and dying out. An anemometer at Blue Hills Observatory in Massachusetts measured gusts up to 180 miles (288 km) before the wind tore it from its mounting.

The storm killed at least 600 people, destroyed more than 9,000 homes, wrecked 26,000 automobiles, and toppled more than 250 million trees.

A storm with the strength of the 1938 hurricane has not pounded New England in six decades. It is, however, just a matter of time before another one strikes. New England has a history of ferocious, although infrequent, hurricanes. One with a path and intensity almost identical to the 1938 hurricane struck in 1815. It ravaged New England, pulverizing the wooden wharves in harbors, and laying to waste fields and forests throughout the region. Another equally violent hurricane hit in 1635, a mere 15 years after the arrival of the Pilgrims at Plymouth Rock.

Today New England is better prepared for the fury of the next devastating hurricane than it was for earlier ones. Satellite and computer technology allows meteorologists to track storms and predict their courses. Storm barriers and dams built after 1938 minimize damage from raging tides, storm surges, and rain-swollen rivers in some parts of the region. These protective measures should reduce the death toll and some of the devastation of major hurricanes. However, the next violent storm may destroy even more property. Since 1938, development along New England's exposed coastline has soared. Bigger and more expensive houses have replaced older summer cottages. And there are more of them. These buildings will be at the mercy of the sea if they ever face a tempest like the storm of 1938.

Residents of the central United States rarely face hurricanes, but encounter a different, less predictable threat—tornadoes.

CHAPTER 7

The 1925 Tri-State Tornado

L ate spring and early summer are tornado season in the central United States. Warm, moist air masses blowing in from the Gulf of Mexico and cold, dry air sweeping in from the Arctic fuel the violent storms that produce tornadoes. When the vastly different air masses collide, the turbulence begins. Warm air streaks upward while cold air streams in from all sides to replace it. A narrow line of thunderclouds develops. Rain and hail beat down, accompanied by streaks of lightning and crashes of thunder.

About one percent of the thunderstorms possess the right conditions for the

The Tri-State Tornado tore through Missouri, Illinois, and Indiana, destroying everything in its path and leaving heaps of rubble behind.

formation of a tornado. The in-rushing air starts to spin fiercely around a small center of low pressure. The winds closest to the center spin the fastest. The spiraling air forms a funnel that swoops down from the thundercloud. Like a giant vacuum cleaner, the funnel sucks up nearly everything in its path. Dirt and debris caught up in the funnel give the twister its dark color. Some funnels never touch down. Others may reach the ground, rise back up, then dip down again.

Scientists classify tornadoes by their intensity using the Fujita scale, named after the famous tornado scientist Tetsuya Fujita. Most tornadoes fall into categories F0 and F1. They generate whirlwind speeds between 40 and 112 miles (64 to 179 km) per hour. These winds inflict light to moderate damage, such as peeling shingles from roofs, tumbling mobile homes from their foundations, and knocking down trees with shallow roots. More significant damage occurs with category F2 and F3 tornadoes. With wind speeds ranging from 113 to 206 miles (180 to 330 km) per hour, these twisters can rip roofs from houses, crush mobile homes, and yank large trees out of the ground. Some can even flip trains over and lift heavy cars into the air. The most powerful tornadoes—category F4 and F5—create wind speeds between 207 and 318 miles (331 to 509 km) per hour. They can smash well-built houses, turn cars into large missiles, and lift small buildings off their foundations.

In Murphysboro, 70 blocks burned in the wake of the tornado. Homeowners saved what they could.

Most tornadoes last a few minutes. Traveling at 30 miles (48 km) per hour, they cut a path of destruction about 150 feet (45 m) wide and a couple of miles (several km) long. However, extremely destructive tornadoes may endure for an hour or more and travel at 60 miles (96 km) per hour. Their damage paths can be more than 1 mile (1.6 km) wide and 60 miles (96 km) long.

In the early afternoon of March 18, 1925, the longest-lasting and deadliest individual tornado in history whipped through portions of three states. Dubbed the Tri-State Tornado, the twister made its debut in eastern Missouri. It roared across the Mississippi

River into southern Illinois, where it did its most lethal work, and then wound down in Indiana. In a three and a half hour rampage the tornado slammed through town after town, advancing faster than any tornado had been known to travel.

The *Literary Digest* described the strange experience of W.E. Lemley, who worked for a lumber company in Poplar Bluff, Missouri. Lemley was "in a restaurant eating when the tornado struck. 'The roof went off first,' he said, 'and then all four sides were swept away. I was left sitting on the floor with nothing around me....'"[1]

James Howard of Murphysboro, Illinois, remembered the twister, too: "I was in the third grade and my teacher told us to stand against the inside wall of our classroom. As the tornado approached I looked out the window. A Model T Ford was parked in front of a grocery store. The wind blew the car backward down the street and an electric pole fell on top of it."[2]

The storm cloud that produced the Tri-State Tornado was so close to the ground that the funnel was not visible. To onlookers, the cloaked tornado appeared to be a seething black fog rolling across the plain.

Mary Belle Melvin of Murphysboro was an eight-year-old student at Lincoln School at the time: "Afternoon recess was cut short because of a black-looking cloud. The windows began to break and my teacher sent us into the hallway. Afterwards, when it had stopped raining we were dismissed from school. The teachers warned us to watch for downed electrical wires.

"On the way home I climbed over an uprooted tree and saw a shoe with a foot in it. As I approached my house, I noticed the roof from the house across the alley leaning against a tree in my backyard. The four sides of the house were laid flat like a house of cards.

"My house was still standing but the roof had been blown off and the windows were broken. We couldn't stay there. So my mother took my two brothers, my sister, and me to a nearby church where we spent the night.

"Coal-burning or wood-burning stoves heated many of the buildings in Murphysboro. When the tornado destroyed some of these buildings, it knocked over the stoves and started many fires.

"About two blocks from the church was a street filled with saloons. The street had

> " The windows began to break and my teacher sent us into the hallway."

Stunned residents of De Soto, Illinois, mill around the ruins of the local elementary school, where 38 students lost their lives, and many others suffered serious injuries.

been particularly hard hit by the tornado but many people had taken shelter in the basements. Now the people were trapped in the basements by debris, and the fire spread to them before they could be rescued. I could hear their screams as the smoke and flames reached them."[3]

Gladys Wheatly Whipkey was a resident of nearby DeSoto, the tornado's next stop. She was thirteen years old: "I was in the schoolyard jumping rope during recess. My mother, who was a teacher in my school, saw the tornado approach. She rang the bell, the signal to come inside. I was upset because recess had ended so early. When I was halfway up the interior stairway the wind blew the door shut, pinning one of my classmates. Then the stairwell collapsed and falling bricks struck me. I was knocked out until the next day.

"The tornado ripped through the building, killing about twenty children, including my cousin Joe. His second-grade classroom had sustained the worst damage of all the rooms. My two younger brothers were in the school, too, but they were unhurt. Initially

The town of Griffin, Indiana, one of the tornado's final stops, was flattened by the twister. Rescuers dug through the rubble, hoping to find survivors.

my mother appeared to be fine, but a few days later she discovered that she had broken a bone in her hand.

"We lived a couple blocks from the school. My father was at home when the tornado whipped through it. Our house collapsed around him. Dazed, he raced to the school to see what happened to the rest of us."[4]

The tornado killed 118 men, women, and children in DeSoto. It carried some of the victims' bodies 1½ miles (2.4 km) before dumping them. One of the more fortunate residents of DeSoto was a young mother who was resting in bed with her two-week-old infant. Her house caved in around her but the support beams fell across the bed in such a way that they missed both mother and child.

The twister's next destination was Frankfort, where it flattened the city. After slashing through several more small towns in Illinois, the tornado picked up speed, crossed

Faced with widespread devastation, rescue workers in Griffin set up tents and began the long process of recovery.

into Indiana, and tore through Griffin and Owensville. It finally died outside of Princeton, where it sucked four miners from a moving car and safely deposited them alongside the road. During its 219-mile (350 km) journey, the twister killed 689 people and injured three times as many.

In the days that followed, as the survivors buried their dead, thousands of sightseers flocked to the devastated area to see the bizarre impact of the storm. Among the curiosities the tornado left behind:

- a barber's chair that had been dumped upright in a field
- a railroad bridge that was pushed 6 feet (1.8 m) from its pillars
- a grain elevator that was lifted from its foundation and moved 40 feet (12 m) without any apparent damage
- a live chicken that had all its feathers plucked off by the wind.

Except for the unusual condition of the sky, residents of the communities devastated by the 1925 Tri-State Tornado had no warning of the coming terror. Today meteorologists using satellite technology and radar can predict the paths of storms likely to generate tornadoes. If weather conditions indicate that a tornado will probably develop, the National Weather Service issues a tornado watch for the threatened region. The purpose of the watch is to make residents alert to ominous changes in the sky. When a tornado is actually detected, the Weather Service broadcasts the location of the twister. In addition, many communities have warning sirens. But, sometimes tornadoes spring up so rapidly there is no time for a warning.

If you see a tornado approaching, notice a sudden, violent wind, or hear a tornado warning for your area, seek shelter immediately. The best place is in a storm cellar or in a basement under sturdy furniture. If your home lacks a basement, seek refuge in a closet, bathroom, or hallway on the lowest level of the house near its center. Stay away from windows. Mobile homes offer little protection against tornado winds. If you live in a mobile home, go to the designated community shelter. If there is none, take cover in a sturdy building or in a ditch.

If you are in a school or other public building when a tornado approaches, head for the designated shelter area. If none exists, take shelter in an interior hallway on the lowest level. If you are caught outside and can't reach a sturdy building, stretch out flat in a ditch or ravine, with your face down and your hands behind your head.

Despite advance warnings, tornadoes continue to kill and maim. Many of the victims never hear the warning, others don't take it seriously. If you hear a tornado warning or observe ominous weather conditions, take cover. It could make the difference between your life and death.

In 1974, a scourge of tornadoes tore through the central United States in the country's worst tornado outbreak ever. While advance warnings saved many lives, the death toll was still unacceptably high.

CHAPTER 8

A Plague of Tornadoes: The 1974 Tornado Outbreak

Τhe most extensive tornado outbreak to ravage the United States was a swarm of 148 separate twisters that were spawned by the same storm system on April 3 and 4, 1974. During its 16-hour rampage the murderous storm roared across the central United States from the Gulf of Mexico to Canada. Thirteen states east of the Mississippi and the Canadian province of Ontario suffered devastation. The average path for each tornado measured 16 miles (26 km), but laid end to end their collective tracks added up to 2,500 miles (4,000 km).

Meteorologists saw the outbreak coming. Although they could not predict exactly

Meteorologists predicted the 1974 tornado outbreak, but did not know exactly where the twisters would touch down. This dark funnel cloud was spotted in Saylor Park, a suburb of Cincinnati, Ohio.

where the twisters would hit, they issued urgent warnings for residents of the dozen Great Plains states known as Tornado Alley. Despite the warnings, 315 people died and 5,500 suffered injuries. The tornadoes hopscotched through America's heartland, dropping down to the ground, wreaking havoc, and vanishing almost as soon as they began.

The most devastated city was Xenia, Ohio, where Jay Smith was a police and fire dispatcher and a member of the police auxiliary. As he recalled, sheer luck saved his life:

"I was patrolling in a police cruiser with a regular police officer and I saw the funnel cloud forming. The tornado passed directly in front of us, missing the cruiser by 300 to 400 yards [270 to 360 m]. The funnel was about ½ mile [0.8 km] wide and coal black. Wood, shingles, and other debris swirled around the cloud like buzzards circling a carcass. The biggest chunks appeared to be 2 or 3 feet [60 to 90 cm] across. The twister sounded like several trains traveling by at the same time. It took about three or four minutes to pass us. As it swooped toward the center of town the funnel grew bigger.

"Over the two-way radio we heard a police supervisor describe what he saw as the tornado bore down on him. The supervisor was in the business district and he called off the street names as the tornado demolished them. He was sitting alone in a cruiser. When the tornado reached him, he shouted, 'A two-by-four just come through my windshield! I've got to get down.' Then there was silence.

"We thought the supervisor was dead but a few minutes later we heard his voice again. He was directing police officers to where they were most needed. He told us to go to the center of town but we couldn't reach it. Crumpled cars and the remains of buildings blocked the streets.

"Near us the twister had flattened a grocery store, a used car lot, a McDonald's, several small stores, and the Red Barn restaurant. All that remained of the Red Barn were the steel girders and the walk-in cooler. The manager of the Red Barn ran toward us waving the money from the cash register and asked if she could sit in the backseat of our cruiser. As she got in, she explained that she had ushered all the employees and customers into the cooler because she knew it would be the safest place. She had saved them all.

> "…she had ushered all the employees and customers into the cooler because she knew it would be the safest place."

Opposite: Although the tornado stripped away the wall of this home in Xenia, Ohio, objects inside the house—including pictures on the walls—remained virtually untouched.

"She told us that there was someone badly hurt in front of the restaurant. We rushed there and found two truckers. One was unharmed, but the other was cut so badly you could see the inside of his abdomen. Surprisingly there was little blood. It was raining so his fellow trucker was building a tent around him using debris and the canvas cover used to protect the load on the truck. I thought this man was going to die because we didn't have the equipment to save him. It took about 45 minutes for an ambulance to arrive. Amazingly, the man survived." [1]

The towering black funnel cloud had cut a swath 3 miles (5 km) long and ½ mile (0.8 km) wide through Xenia. In five minutes it had reduced half the town to splinters. The twister wrenched buildings from foundations, uprooted trees, and even

After rummaging through the wreckage of his Xenia home, this man recovered two items of sentimental value—a scrapbook and lamp base.

hurled the back cars of a freight train onto Main Street. About 1,000 of the town's residents suffered injuries and 34 people died. Of the town's twelve schools, six sustained severe damage or were reduced to rubble. Fortunately, most of the students had already left for the day, but not all.

Ruth Venuti, 18, was waiting at Xenia High School for a friend to give her a ride home. In the distance she noticed an immense black cloud change into a gigantic, rotating funnel. Ruth realized a tornado was headed her way. She raced to the auditorium to alert drama club members rehearsing for an upcoming performance of *The Boyfriend*. Bursting in on the rehearsal, Ruth asked if anybody wanted to see a tornado.

David Heath, an English teacher and the club's director, jumped off the stage and told the students to follow. They dashed to the hallway, where through the windows they spied an enormous funnel writhing just 200 feet (61 m) away. Terrified, the group took cover in the school's central corridor. Seconds later the tornado struck. For four minutes, mud, wood, dirt, broken glass, and other chunks of debris swirled above the students, who were now lying on the floor.

None of the students was killed or seriously injured. But the twister had obliterated the top floor of the school and partially caved in the auditorium roof. Sprawled across the stage where the students had rehearsed only minutes earlier was an upside-down school bus.

CHAPTER 9

The Blizzard of 1888

Howling winds, blinding snows, and piercing cold temperatures characterize blizzards. Like hurricanes and tornadoes, the collision of a warm, moist air mass with a cold, dry one sparks these powerful storms. Blizzards usually occur in late winter, frequently after a spell of warm weather. Frigid air from the Arctic slinks down into the temperate zone—usually over central Canada and the Midwest—and faces off with warm, humid air advancing northward from the tropics. The frigid, heavy air forces the warm air ahead of it to rise. As the warm air rises into the cold air, it cools and the water vapor in it condenses. However, because the water vapor is wrung out at temperatures below freezing, ice crystals form, not water droplets. The ice crystals clump together to form snowflakes.

The Blizzard of 1888 coated the elevated rails in New York City with ice, trapping 15,000 passengers in train cars high above the street.

Strong winds give blizzards their ferociousness. To be categorized as a blizzard, a snowfall must have winds that blow at a sustained speed of at least 35 miles (56 km) per hour for a minimum of three hours. The temperature must plunge to a bone-chilling 10°F (−12°C) or lower, and visibility must be reduced to less than 1,500 feet (455 m).

One of the most memorable blizzards in America's history took the Northeast by surprise more than a century ago. On the weekend of March 10 and 11, 1888, spring was in the air. In New York City, crocuses had already bloomed and robins had returned from their winter habitats. The forecast for that Sunday called for cloudy weather followed by light rain, then clearing. Yet few people were concerned on Sunday afternoon when heavy rains drenched the city.

Shortly after midnight, the cold air arrived. Temperatures plummeted. The steady torrent of rain changed to snow, and the snow fell at the extraordinary rate of 1 inch (2.5 cm) an hour during the next 15 hours.

On Monday morning, parents bundled up their children and sent them off to school. But on this day, some schools never opened, and the rest closed early. So children who had just trudged in the bitter cold and traversed snowdrifts larger than themselves were compelled to turn around and retrace their steps.

Katherine Ward Fisher wrote about her younger sister's experiences in a letter: "[My sister] started for public school but soon turned back. My mother, not realizing the severity of the storm, started her off again. This time she fell in a drift and could not get up. A man picked her up and brought her home."[1]

Adults did not fare any better. Working people, worried that they would lose their jobs if they stayed home, braved the storm's fury. Most regretted their decision. Businesses closed early for lack of customers, sending their workers home. But by then more snow had fallen, the wind was blowing more fiercely, and the temperature was still dropping.

A writer for the *New York Evening Sun* made a curious observation: "So fierce was the wind that sparrows could not fly against it. They rested in the windows of THE SUN Building, and started out against the air to stand still with wings fluttering vainly. If they attempted to fly [with the wind] they were hustled along like stones thrown with fearful force."[2]

The blizzard dumped snow in a wide swath from Maryland to Maine, and over the Atlantic. At sea, the storm created a dangerous mix of snow, churning swells, and frigid gales gusting as fast as 90 miles (144 km) per hour. About 200 boats and ships were

either sunk, grounded, or wrecked, with the loss of at least 100 mariners.

On land, ice and wind brought telephone and telegraph lines crashing down. There was no way to communicate between cities that conditions were worsening. (Radio and television had not yet been invented.) Hundreds of trains were stopped dead in their tracks, blocked by immense snowdrifts up to 30 feet (9 m) high. Travelers were able to sit in the comfort of warm train cars until the coal for the heating stoves ran out. When the fuel was gone the temperatures inside the trains plunged. Passengers stranded close to towns tramped through thigh-high snow to reach shelter.

In New York City, the transportation system ground to a halt. Unwilling to risk the lives of their animals, operators of horse-drawn streetcars and cabs stopped operations. Ice-coated rails were the downfall of the elevated commuter trains. Unable to move on the slippery tracks, the trains trapped 15,000 passengers high above the streets in unheated cars. On the ground, enterprising men furnished ladders and some charged passengers as much as two dollars each for the privilege of climbing down. (The fare for the ride on the elevated railroad had been just a nickel!)

Meanwhile, would-be passengers trekked from station to station looking for a way home. Exhausted and cold from fighting the wind and the mountains of snow, some men and women simply collapsed into snowdrifts, too tired to move. About 200 persons froze to death in the streets of New York. More would have met the same fate except for the effort made by New York City policemen to rescue people from drifts.

One frustrated New Yorker made it all the way home only to find that he could not reach his own front door. His story was recounted in "Snow Bound on His Own Doorstep," an article published in the *New York Evening Sun*: "An unfortunate man who lives in one of the houses that sit far back from the walk on the south side of Fifty-third street, near Seventh avenue, when he got within sight of home late Monday afternoon, found a drift as high as his head covering all his sidewalk. He attacked it valiantly, and was buried at the third step. He floundered out and stood off a way to consider the situation. Then he tried to flank the drift by hugging the fence, which was iron and very cold. While he was wrestling with the fence his wife saw him from the window. She threw it up and with the children stood there shouting shrill encouragement to the man. Thus inspired he put new life into his struggle, and got himself two feet [0.6 m] deeper into the drift. The neighbors came to their windows and looked on, too. Finally he backed out and held a consultation with his wife to the aspects of affairs. At her suggestion he

Opposite: The blizzard damaged telephone and telegraph wires in New York City and throughout the Northeast. Communication between cities became impossible.

Snowdrifts more than ten feet (3 m) high accumulated outside some homes and businesses. New York City firefighters and police officers rescued many victims during the storm.

climbed the fence into a neighbor's yard and then climbed the neighbor's fence into his own and so finally got into the bosom of his family." [3]

Twelve-year-old Milton Daub lived in the South Bronx section of New York City. At that time his neighborhood consisted of farms, estates, and small houses. For Milton the blizzard turned out to be a gold mine. Years later, he wrote about his experience in an essay: "On the morning of March 12th 1888 . . . snow was piled up to the windows one story high, our front and back doors were blocked with snow, all windows were covered. Mother had the lamps lit.

"My father said to my mother, '. . . How are we fixed with food?'

"'We have plenty of everything, all we need is some milk.'

"Father said, 'I hope that someone will try to get around and sell us some condensed milk. . . .'

"In public school we were taught how different people thru out [*sic*] the world travel about, those living in the far North, where there is plenty of snow... travel with snow shoes, to carry merchandise... a sledge and dogs are used... I mentioned this to my father....

"When I finished talking, he said, '...We have no snow shoes in this house...'

"My answer was, 'I will make a pair of snow shoes.'

"[Using] two wooden barrel hoops, some wire, some twine, piece of canvas, and my roller skates without the wheels... my father and myself had a pair of home made snow shoes....

"...Father nailed a box on top of my sledge, [the] sledge and snow shoes were placed outside of the window, one story high, father brought the close [sic] line, [and] tied one end around my waist, then I stepped out of the window, placing my feet on the roller skates...."

Milton practiced walking atop the snowdrift with the snowshoes on. After several minutes his parents were convinced that he would not sink down into the snow.

According to Milton: "No doubt I was a funny sight to every one who seen [sic] me walking, still every one was anxious to have me buy milk for them.... I bought 50 cts worth of condensed milk at Mike Ash's grocery store, Mr. Ash charged me the regular price, I sold the milk at the same amount, at every delivery I received a fine reward... in less than twenty minutes I had tips up to $2.00. I also had my original 50 cts...."

Milton returned to the store, bought a case of milk, sold it, earned more tips, and repeated the process again and again. He was away from home for nearly three hours. When he finally returned, his worried parents scolded him. Then they saw his tips and wanted to know if he had overcharged the neighbors. Milton assured them that he had not. After eating, he went back out.

By 3:00 PM Milton had sold all of Mr. Ash's milk, so he bought a case at a different store. Milton also helped a woman get a prescription filled for her sick husband, and he delivered groceries for some people. Around 5:00 PM Milton bought two loaves of bread for his family for ten cents and returned home, exhausted.

Milton recalled: "I felt very proud, this is the first time in my young life that I am paying for bread, with money that I had earned."[4]

> "I felt very proud, this is the first time in my young life that I am paying for bread, with money that I had earned."

In the aftermath of the blizzard, crews worked to remove snow from the streets surrounding Times Square.

After supper Milton gave his mother his tips and then fell fast asleep. He had earned $67.65. In today's money that is worth about eight hundred dollars!

Temperatures dropped further that evening, and by midnight on Monday, they had reached 8°F (–13°C). By Tuesday morning, they were an even more frigid –5°F (–21°C). But by Tuesday afternoon the snow had stopped falling and the digging out began.

In "The City Snowed Under," the *New York Evening Sun* described how the city struggled with the aftermath of the storm: "It was all new to New Yorkers. Here were men tunnelling through drifts higher than their heads to clean the sidewalks; there were others shovelling their way to

Some residents and businesses paid outrageous fees to have their homes and stores dug out.

the wagon ways to get out of their houses; elsewhere were letter carriers bawling to people in doors to come out over ten-foot [3 m] snow heaps to get their letters. Then there were schoolhouses, not open in two days, walled apart from the children by insurmountable ranges of snow, parks that no one had entered, streets that no wagon could traverse, and shops whose fronts were fortified against their owners." [5]

In 1888, several blizzards just as formidable struck other parts of the United States. These blizzards impacted mainly rural areas, where people were more accustomed to major snowfalls. This one, however, became famous because it overwhelmed the major cities along the eastern seaboard, causing anxiety, uncertainty, and death.

The total breakdown in communications prompted New York City and other urban areas to run telephone, telegraph, and power lines beneath the streets, where they would be safe from storms. To weatherproof their transportation systems, some cities built subways—underground railroads. Boston opened the first one in America in 1897.

Unfortunately, with the growing dependency on the automobile, transportation in urban areas today is just as vulnerable to blizzards as it was in the late 1800s. The city of Buffalo, New York, learned this the hard way.

CHAPTER 10

The Buffalo Blizzard of 1977

Buffalo, the second largest city in New York State, endures the worst winter weather of any major metropolitan area in the United States. The city stretches alongside the eastern edge of Lake Erie. Because of its location, Buffalo catches moisture-laden winds blowing off the lake, much of which remains unfrozen during winter. In a typical year Buffalo receives about 8 feet (2.4 m) of snow altogether. As a result, the 1.5 million people residing in the metropolitan Buffalo area have learned to expect snow in winter and to deal with it.

However, in the winter of 1976–77 the snows started early, in October, and by the

After five days of a raging blizzard in January 1977, motorists in Buffalo, New York, faced the daunting task of locating their vehicles and digging them out.

fourth week of January nearly twice the annual snowfall had already fallen. On the morning of January 27, 1977, the worst blizzard in the city's history blew off the lake with little warning. Nearly 3 feet (0.9 m) of snow from previous storms still covered the ground when the blizzard struck. Over a five-day period 12 more inches (30 cm) of snow fell. Frigid winds reaching 85 miles (136 km) per hour stirred up snow on the ground and mingled it with freshly falling snow. The winds created immense snow-drifts up to 30 feet (9 m) high and generated a numbing windchill factor that descended as low as minus 60°F (–51°C). Winds this cold can freeze human skin in as little as a minute.

"...even the Buffalo Police Department wasn't prepared for a storm of this severity."

Most schools had already closed, but the storm stranded 17,000 workers in their downtown offices. Thousands of motorists abandoned their automobiles when the roads became impassable. Most of the stranded motorists took shelter where they could find it. Others waited to be rescued. Despite such severe and unexpected weather conditions, only nine people froze to death in their cars.

Chief Larry Ramunno of the Buffalo Police Department was part of a rescue team that braved perilous conditions to rescue nine other stranded travelers from the same fate. According to Chief Ramunno: "The Skyway Bridge, which runs alongside Lake Erie, is one of the most dangerous places to be in Buffalo during a blizzard. The winds whip the snow so fiercely up there that you can't see 2 feet [0.6 m] in front of you. At the start of the big blizzard, the Buffalo Police Department closed the Skyway's entrances, unaware that nine travelers were trapped on the bridge.

"That evening around 9:30, a police dispatcher received a call from a concerned citizen. The citizen had noticed a flare burning on the Skyway. We then realized that at least one motorist was stranded up there. My precinct was four blocks from the base of the bridge. So I volunteered along with two other patrolmen to make the rescue. We knew our cruisers were no match for the deep snow. We would have to make the rescue on foot.

"Winter in Buffalo is as predictable as the weather in Florida. In Florida you expect the sun to shine. In Buffalo you expect snow to fly. But even the Buffalo Police Department wasn't prepared for a storm of this severity. We didn't have uniforms that could protect us from the elements. So local radio stations broadcast our urgent appeal for the equipment that we needed. Some citizens lent us their ski masks and rock-climbing outfits—insulated jumpsuits that covered our entire bodies. The community really came together.

"The winds on the Skyway were strong enough to blow a person off the bridge. So the three of us linked ourselves together with a thick rope. Breaking a path through the snow was hard work and walking into the wind wasn't much easier. We gripped the railings on the bridge to keep from being blown away. The cold air stung our eyes and lungs. Ice crystals formed around the openings of our ski masks.

Buffalo schoolchildren had a long holiday following the blizzard. Schools remained closed for nearly two weeks.

"Eventually we came upon three cars but we couldn't see inside them even when we brushed off the snow. Condensation from the moist breath of the occupants had frosted the windows. We kicked the snow away from the doors of the first car and opened them. Inside we found five people huddled together. They were in shock. Even though the engine was running and the heater was on, they were so cold they couldn't move. The next car held four more people, all shivering and in about the same state as the ones in the first vehicle. The third car had broken down so its occupants had moved into the other two cars.

"Because the winds would have blown the people off the bridge, we had brought another rope and tied it around their waists. Retracing our footsteps, we led them back to the station house and gave them coffee and donuts. Even though they thought they would never warm up, they all did. Not one person developed frostbite."[1]

Larry Ramunno's assignment that night was not a high-tech rescue. It was straightforward operation that simply involved three brave men willing to risk their lives to save others.

While police officers and firefighters had their hands full rescuing people, Jerry Aqualina, the general curator of the Buffalo Zoo, had his own worries: How could the

The blizzard caused emergency conditions throughout the Buffalo area. U.S. Marines used helicopters, and donned snowshoes, to deliver food and supplies.

zookeepers feed and care for the animals if they couldn't even reach the cages? "We needed to feed all one thousand animals in the zoo. Normally we divided this chore among fifteen zookeepers. But because of the storm, only four or five zookeepers were on the job from the outset. Snow 8 feet [2.4 m] deep covered all the access roads within the zoo and the entrances to the outside exhibits. So we used sleds to reach the exhibits. Then we tossed the food up and over the snowdrifts to get it into the exhibits. Obtaining fresh fruits and vegetables for the animals was difficult because the outside roads remained closed. But we had a good supply of hay and grain, as well as a freezer full of meat.

"No animals starved to death but the severe drop in temperature and the windchill proved too much for some. We lost a Markhor, which is a goat from Asia, a peré david deer, some antelope, and a ratlike creature called a nutria. The frigid temperatures, however, hurt the waterbirds the most and many died, including two beautiful black swans.

Opposite: The task of clearing snow-blocked highways and streets was complicated by thousands of abandoned vehicles.

"Nevertheless, the biggest problem we experienced at the Buffalo Zoo was animal escapes. We use moats and 8-foot-high [2.4 m] fences to separate our animals from the public. But snow piled up so high at the grazing animal exhibits that the animals could walk up the drifts and over the fence. A male and two female reindeer got loose.

"We found the male near the zoo and captured it safely using a dart with a tranquilizing drug. But the two females took us on a merry chase. With the help of the community we located one female on a small side street. We successfully lassoed her and tied her up until the vet could give her a drug to calm her.

"Well-meaning people on snowmobiles chased the second female and penned her in. The stress was too much for the animal and she died from shock. She was pregnant so we lost the baby she was carrying, too.

"Two of our mouflon sheep escaped from the children's zoo. These are wild sheep from southern Europe. We recovered one but the other disappeared without a trace.

"To prevent even more escapes, we decided to dig a moat around the perimeter of the exhibits, as most animals will not cross a moat. This was a formidable task because several of the exhibits were longer than a football field. The snow was 8 feet [2.4 m] deep and the moats needed to be 7 feet [2.1 m] wide. The bison were accustomed to the zookeepers so we could dig in their exhibit areas without fear of attack. But some of the other animals needed to be locked in their barns. This meant digging our way to the barns first to open the doors.

"I don't know how the rumor started, but the media reported that our polar bears got loose. The bear exhibits are located in an area protected from the wind and drifting snow. We got calls from a lot of nervous residents, but there never was any danger of bears going free." [2]

For the people of Buffalo, cleaning up after the storm posed almost a greater challenge than surviving it. On highways and roads everywhere, cars were completely buried, hindering snowplowing efforts. Drifts were packed so high and so deep in places that normal snow removal equipment could not excavate them. To make matters worse, 33 out of the 79 snowplows in Buffalo's snow removal arsenal had been damaged in earlier storms and were out of commission. So officials summoned private contractors, volunteer firefighters, the Army Corps of Engineers, and National Guard and Army troops, as well as the Marines, to help in the battle against the snow. By February 14, most roads had been cleared and schools reopened.

PART 3

Water: Too Much, Too Little

What do you think of when you hear the word *water*—sparkling lakes, bubbling brooks, raindrops, a liquid to drink? How about killer floods? Water, one of the most basic substances on Earth, has a murderous side. When too much rain falls and water-soaked land cannot absorb any more, water spills into already swollen streams and rivers. Some waterways turn into wild, swirling currents and escape the confines of their banks. Roaring downstream they sweep away cars, houses, and even bridges.

While too much water can kill, so can too little. To survive, the typical adult needs to drink about 1 quart (1 L) of water a day. Additional water is necessary to support the crops and animals that humans depend on for their food. Although water is plentiful on Earth, most of it is found in the salty oceans and is useless for drinking or farming.

Only three percent of our planet's water supply is freshwater. It comes from rain and snowfall, and some places receive more of it than others. Occasionally weather patterns shift and a region that typically experiences little precipitation may be deluged. And a place where rain typically falls may experience a drought, an extended dry spell.

When too little precipitation falls over a long period, streams, rivers, and lakes begin to dry up. In forests, dead trees become parched, and ready to ignite if lightning strikes. Dry winds fan the flames. In farmlands, extended droughts can kill crops and create food shortages.

Ocean phenomena known as El Niño and La Niña are responsible for some of the world's greatest weather upheavals. An El Niño is a massive pool of abnormally warm water and a La Niña is a massive pool of unusually cold water. Both form in the western central Pacific, but not at the same time. An El Niño makes its appearance about every three to ten years, around Christmastime. Ocean currents in the western central Pacific shift direction. They push warm water eastward toward South America, raising temperatures across the ocean. This massive surge of heated water warms and affects the flow of air above it, reshaping weather patterns across much of the globe. A powerful El Niño can produce torrential rains in California and along the usually arid west coast of South America. At the same time, drought is likely to occur in Hawaii, Australia, and Indonesia. An El Niño usually lasts 12 to 18 months. The most destructive El Niño of the twentieth century appeared in 1982 and 1983. Flash floods and killer mudslides plagued Chile and Peru. Hundreds perished and thousands lost their homes. A La Niña brings extreme changes in weather, too. It can create monstrous downpours in Asia and drought in the United States and parts of South America.

Long droughts in industrialized nations, like the United States, usually result in economic hardship for farmers and higher food prices for consumers. But in developing nations, where subsistence farmers barely grow enough food during a good year to survive, prolonged droughts can lead to famine and death. Our country's worst experience with prolonged drought occurred in the 1930s in a region of the country dubbed the Dust Bowl.

Drought in the Nation's Breadbasket: The Dust Bowl

The morning of April 14, 1935, began in Kansas with clear blue skies and a warm, gentle southwest breeze—nothing unusual. In the early afternoon, however, birds began to act strangely. They flocked together anxiously on the ground. Suddenly, the sky darkened and a black cloud thousands of feet high filled the northwest horizon. Although it looked to some like a seething tide of muddy water, the cloud contained no moisture. It bore thousands of tons of topsoil and clay, swept from the bone-dry fields of the Great Plains.

Traveling at speeds up to 70 miles (112 km) an hour, the dust cloud rolled over

On Black Sunday—April 14, 1935—mountainous clouds of dust blew across the Great Plains, turning day into night.

Kansas, Colorado, and Oklahoma like a dry tsunami. It stalled cars, suffocated cattle, and piled up against barns, houses, and fences. The rubbing together of billions of dirt particles created static charges that jammed radio signals and produced an eerie glow along the metal edges of fences. Although this day would come to be known as "Black Sunday," residents of the Great Plains were no strangers to dust storms.

Dust Bowl was the name given to the expanse of land stretching across southwestern Kansas, southeastern Colorado, northeastern New Mexico, and the panhandles of Texas and Oklahoma. In this territory, a combination of poor farming and grazing practices and severe drought had stripped the ground of native prairie grasses. Without the grass to anchor the soil and lock in moisture, the topsoil turned to dust and began to blow away.

Much of the Dust Bowl region had been turned into farmland by settlers who came west after the Civil War. In wet years the crops were successful but in dry years the farms were too small to eke out a living. High prices paid for wheat during World War I (1914–18), and an unusual spate of moist weather, encouraged farmers in the Dust Bowl to plant as much wheat as possible. Wheat plants did not protect the soil from wind erosion and the soil began to drift.

The drought began in the Great Plains during the summer of 1931, but the first dust storms didn't appear until 1932. Crops failed and the dust began to fly. The next year the drought extended over a greater area and the crop failures and dust storms spread. The drought continued for another four years, into 1937. As the crops failed, farmers, unable to pay their bills, lost their farms. Most of the displaced farmers packed up and headed west to California.

One of the settlers who lived in the Dust Bowl was Caroline A. Henderson. Mrs. Henderson had moved from Iowa to Oklahoma in 1906 to take up farming. She wrote the following essay in April 1935 to explain the hardships brought on by drought: "...We are in the worst of the dust storm area where...[the] expression 'dust to eat' is not merely a figure of speech...but the phrasing of a bitter reality, increasing in seriousness with each passing day...."

Drought gripped the Dust Bowl from 1931 to 1937. Insufficient rainfall, combined with poor farming methods, caused topsoil to turn to dust, ruining crops and destroying farms.

"There are days when for hours at a time we cannot see the windmill fifty feet [15 m] from the kitchen door. There are days when for briefer periods one cannot distinguish the windows from the solid wall because of the solid blackness of the raging storm. . . .This wind-driven dust, fine as finest flour, penetrates wherever air can go.

"After one such storm, I scraped up a dustpanful of this pulverized soil in the first preliminary cleaning of the bathtub! . . . A friend writes of attending dinner where 'the guests were given wet towels to spread over their faces so they could breathe.' At the little country store . . . after one of the worst of these storms, the candies in the showcase all looked alike and equally brown, but the girls blew and shook until [the candies] looked quite bright again! 'Dust to eat,' and dust to breathe and dust to drink. Dust in the beds and in the flour bin, on dishes and walls and windows, in hair and eyes and ears and teeth and throats, to say nothing of the heaped-up accumulation on floors and window sills after one of the bad days.

> **"Dust in the beds and in the flour bin, on dishes and walls and windows, in hair and eyes and ears and teeth and throats..."**

"Yet these personal inconveniences are of slight moment as compared with the larger effects of the persistent drought and wind erosion. . . . Since 1931 the record has been one of practically unbroken drought resulting in complete exhaustion of subsoil moisture, the stripping of our fields of all protective covering, and the progressive pulverization of the surface soil . . . we realize that some farmers have themselves contributed to this reaping of the whirlwind. Under the stimulus of wartime prices and the humanizing of agriculture through the use of tractors and improved machinery, large areas of buffalo grass and blue stem pasture lands were broken out for wheat raising. . . .

"Now we are facing a fourth year of failure. There can be no wheat for us in 1935 in spite of all our careful and expensive work in preparing the ground, sowing, and resowing our allotted acreage. Native grass pastures are . . . in many cases hopelessly ruined, smothered under by drifted sand. Fences are buried under banks of thistles and hard-packed earth or undermined by the eroding action of the wind and lying flat on the ground. Less traveled roads are impassable, covered deep under sand or the finer silt-like loam. Orchards, groves, and hedge-rows, cultivated for many years with patient care, are dead or dying. . . .

Many farm families were reluctant to leave home for fear of being caught in a dust storm. These people, seeking shelter from the dust, ran past a barn partially buried in a drift.

"...the longing for rain has become almost an obsession. We remember the gentle all-night rains that used to make a grateful music on the shingles close above our heads, or the showers that came just in time to save a dying crop. We recall the torrents that occasionally burst upon us in sudden storms, making our level farm a temporary lake where only the ducks felt at home. We dream of...the fresh green of sprouting wheat or barley, the reddish bronze of springing rye. But we awaken to another day of wind and dust and hopes deferred...."[1]

To combat the problems of the Dust Bowl, the federal government created the Soil Conservation Service (SCS) in 1935. Agricultural experts from the SCS showed farmers how to minimize soil loss by building terraces, plowing along contour lines, and replacing wheat crops with soil-conserving grasses and legumes. Trees and shrubs were planted as windbreaks. By the early 1940s the conditions for the Dust Bowl no longer existed. However, someday they will return.

Climate experts have evidence that even more severe droughts have stricken the

Great Plains during the past 10,000 years. These megadroughts turned vast stretches of land into sandy deserts with shifting dunes like those found in the deserts of Africa. The dunes still exist in the Great Plains but they are covered by a thin layer of grass or sagebrush, and appear to be hills. The largest area of sand dunes in the United States is found in a region of Nebraska appropriately called the Sand Hills. The next megadrought will kill the vegetation protecting the dunes and once again turn the land into a great desert of drifting sand.

While you cannot prevent a drought, you can conserve water if you live in a drought-prone region. Here are some tips for reducing water consumption inside your home:

- Take short showers.
- Turn off the water while brushing your teeth.
- Keep a bottle of drinking water in your refrigerator instead of running the faucet until the water is cold enough to drink.
- Rinse fruits and vegetables in a pan and use the waste water to water plants.
- Test your toilet for leaks by adding a few drop of food coloring to the water in the toilet tank. Don't flush. If the color appears in the bowl after a few minutes, it means the toilet leaks and should be repaired.

Forests have adapted to long droughts and the fire that often follows in their wake. However, for people who make their homes in or near forested lands, these fires can be catastrophic.

The Great Peshtigo Fire

Forest fires are as essential to the health of a forest as the sun and rain. The flames clear away the brush and dead branches that pile up on a forest floor, making way for new growth and a greater variety of plant species. Dead wood can remain for years without rotting, trapping minerals within the wood. Fire releases the minerals, enriching the soil and making the minerals available for new growth.

When fire strikes, forest animals follow their instincts. Chipmunks, mice, and other small burrowing creatures run away or seek shelter underground where the soil protects them from the heat. Large mammals such as deer and bear sense the fire and

This map shows a bird's-eye view of Peshtigo as it appeared in 1871 before the fire. The Reverend Pernin's church is labeled 1, and the schoolhouse is labeled 2.

move away from the flames. Animal deaths do occur during conflagrations but the numbers are usually small. Some critters actually face a greater danger once the fire passes. With much of the ground cover gone, small animals lose their hiding places. They make easy targets for hungry hawks and owls. Plant-eating animals may starve because their food supply went up in smoke.

However, plants make a rapid comeback. Regrowth begins almost immediately in moist sites where the flames were not too intense. Roots, bulbs, and stems that survived below the surface send up new shoots through the blackened soil. Within a few years new grasses, shrubs, wildflowers, and saplings can transform a lightly burned area into a lush meadow. However, areas that burned intensely take much longer to recover.

Forest fires become disasters when people and their property lie in their path. The most deadly and destructive forest fire in U.S. history swept through the woods of Wisconsin and Michigan on October 8, 1871. It burned about 4¼ million acres (17,200 sq. km) and destroyed 23 towns and villages. Since the fire reached its greatest intensity in and around the town of Peshtigo, Wisconsin, it was dubbed the Great Peshtigo Fire.

Peshtigo was a typical lumber town, built around a sawmill and surrounded by dense forests. The town's largest employer was the Peshtigo Company, which operated several enterprises including a sawmill with 97 saws, a gristmill, machine shop, and a woodenware factory that produced shingles, tubs, pails, and broom handles. The town was home to about 2,000 people.

The Peshtigo River flowed through Peshtigo on its journey to Lake Michigan's Green Bay, 6 miles (10 km) away. Many of the town's 350 houses lined the riverbank. Not surprisingly, the houses and other buildings in town had been built from wood.

Drought plagued the region in 1871. By early October, many of Peshtigo's residents felt uneasy. For 14 weeks no rain had fallen and many streams had dried up. The pine forests along Green Bay were hazy with smoke from the many small fires that besieged the area. These fires smoldered in the boggy soil and underbrush deep in the woods. They had been set by hunters, lumberjacks, farmers, and railroad workers to clear away stumps and rubble. However, the small blazes appeared to be under control. As an extra precaution Peshtigo's citizens had cleared away all the trees in a wide strip around the town to provide a firebreak.

On Sunday, October 8, a strong wind blew in from the southwest and united the scattered blazes into two immense firestorms deep in the forest. Throughout the day the amount of smoke in Peshtigo increased. And as the smoke increased, so did the anxiety of many of the townspeople, including Reverend Peter Pernin, Peshtigo's Catholic priest.

In an account published in 1874, Reverend Pernin described the events of that afternoon and evening: "The afternoon passed in complete inactivity. I remained ...a prey to the indefinable apprehensions of impending calamity.... Towards seven in the evening...I left home to see how it went with my neighbors. I stepped over first to the house of an elderly kindhearted widow.... My companion was as troubled as myself, and kept pressuring her children to take some precautionary measures, but they refused, laughing lightly at her fears."

A little after 8:00 PM the air in Peshtigo turned unbearably hot. The smoke became so thick it was almost suffocating. The townspeople heard a strange, far-off rumbling noise that they had never heard before. Their uneasiness heightened as the noise grew steadily louder. By 9:00 PM it became a terrible roar.

Father Peter Pernin, the Catholic priest in Peshtigo, witnessed the fire and survived by diving into the river.

Reverend Pernin's lethargy passed and he decided to do something about his fears: "From listless and undecided as I had previously been, I suddenly became active and determined.... I then set about digging a trench six feet [1.8 m] wide and six or seven feet [1.8–2.1 m] deep, in the sandy soil of the garden...."

Then a Mrs. Tyler, another neighbor, approached him. "'Father,' she questioned, 'do you think there is any danger?'

"'I do not know,' was my reply, 'but I have unpleasant presentiments, and feel myself impelled to prepare for trouble.'

"'But if a fire breaks out, Father, what are we to do?'

"'In that case, Madam, seek the river at once.'

"I gave her no reason for advising such a course, perhaps I had really none to offer, beyond that it was my innate conviction. . . .

"After finishing the digging of the trench I placed within it my trunks, books, church ornaments, and other valuables, covering the whole with sand to a depth of about a foot [0.3 m]."

By the time Reverend Pernin finished, the inferno had reached the edge of town. It created updrafts with hurricane-force wind, and these fierce winds then produced flaming whirlwinds—tornadoes of fire. Waves of burning heat swept over Peshtigo. All the buildings burst into flames. The townspeople's worst fears had been realized.

Reverend Pernin's account continued: "I had delayed my departure [for the river] too long. . . . The air was no longer fit to breathe, full as it was of sand, dust, ashes, cinders, sparks, smoke, and fire. It was almost impossible to keep one's eyes unclosed, to distinguish the road, or to recognize people, though the way was crowded with pedestrians, as well as vehicles crossing and crashing against each other in general flight. Some were hastening towards the river, others from it. . . . A thousand discordant deafening noises rose on the air together. The neighing of horses, falling of chimneys, crashing of uprooted trees, roaring and whistling of the wind, crackling of fire as it ran with lightning-like rapidity from house to house—all sounds were there save that of the human voice. People seemed stricken dumb by terror. They jostled each other without exchanging look, word or counsel. . . . We all hurried blindly on to our fate. . . .

"I was . . . thrown down over some motionless object lying on the earth; it proved to be a woman and little girl, both dead. . . . With a long breath I rose to my feet, but only to be hurled down again. . . .

"[When we] arrived near the river, we saw that the houses adjacent to it were on fire, whilst the wind blew the flames and cinders directly into the water. The place was no longer safe. I resolved then to cross to the other side though the bridge was already on fire. The [bridge] presented a scene of indescribable and awful confusion, each [person] thinking he could attain safety on the other side of the river. Those who lived in the east were hurrying towards the west, and those who dwelt in the west were wildly pushing on to the east. . . . [After I arrived] on the other side I resolved to descend [into] the river. . . . The banks of the river as far as the eye could reach were covered with people standing there, motionless as statues, some with eyes staring upturned towards heaven, and tongues protruded. The greater number seemed to have no idea of taking any steps to procure their safety, imagining, as many afterwards acknowledged to me, that the end of the world had arrived and that there was nothing for them but silent submission to their fate. Without uttering a word...I pushed persons standing on each side of me into the water. One of them sprang back again with a half-smothered cry, murmuring, 'I am wet'; but immersion in water was better than immersion in fire. I caught him again and dragged him out with me into the river as far as possible. At the same moment I heard a splash of the water along the river's brink. All had followed my example. It was time; the air was no longer fit for inhalation, whilst the intensity of the heat was increasing....

"It was about ten o'clock when we entered the river.... Once in the water up to our necks, I thought we would at least be safe from fire, but it was not so; the flames darted over the river as they did over land....Our heads were in continual danger. It was only by throwing water constantly over them and our faces and beating the river with our hands that we kept the flames at bay. Clothing and quilts had been thrown into the river, to save them doubtless, and they were floating all around. I caught at some that came within reach and covered with them the heads of the persons who were leaning against or clinging to me. The wraps dried quickly in the furnace-like heat and caught fire whenever we ceased sprinkling them....

"Once in the water up to our necks, I thought we would at least be safe from fire, but it was not so..."

"Not far from me a woman was supporting herself in the water by the means of a log...a cow swam past...[and] overturned...the log to which the woman was clinging and she disappeared into the water. I thought her lost; but soon saw her emerge from it holding on with one hand to the horns of the cow, and throwing water on her head with the other....I was told later that the animal had swum to shore, bearing her human burden safely with her; and what threatened to bring destruction to the woman had proved the means of her salvation....

"Things went well enough with me during the first three or four hours of this prolonged bath [in cold water], owing in part I suppose, to my being continually in

Like the other buildings in Peshtigo, the schoolhouse was made of wood. It burned readily in the inferno.

motion, either throwing water on my own head or on that of my neighbors.

"It was not so, however, with some of those who were standing near me, for their teeth were chattering and their limbs convulsively trembling. . . . Dreading that so long a sojourn in the water might be followed by severe cramps, perhaps death, I endeavored to ascend the bank a short distance, so as to ascertain the temperature, but my shoulders were scarcely out of the river when a voice called to me, 'Father, beware, you are on fire!'

"The hour of deliverance from this prison of fire and water had not yet arrived. . . .

"There is an end to all things here below, even misfortune. The longed-for moment of our return to land was at length arriving, and already sprinkling of our heads was becoming unnecessary. I drew near the bank, seated myself on a log, being in this manner only partly immersed in the water. Here I was seized by a violent chill. A young man perceiving it threw a blanket over me, which at once afforded me relief. And soon after I was able to leave this compulsory bath in which I had plunged for about five hours and a half." [1]

After the firestorm raged through Peshtigo, it raced toward a sawmill on the outskirts of Menomonee, a small town to the northeast. At the mill were a bookkeeper named Elbridge West Meirele, four other men, two women, a six-year-old boy, and a baby belonging to the cook. Little did Mr. Meirele know that he was about to become the baby's salvation.

In a handwritten account, Mr. Meirele later recorded his memories of the Great Peshtigo Fire: "...a magnificent ball of fire, as large as a man's head, was shot like a bomb from the coming fire....[It] struck near the corner of the mill and in a second had ignited all around it...in a moment a hundred similar balls were falling all around and a hundred fires were blazing in the clearing. It was [like a] shower of fire except that the balls did not fall direct from the sky but shot over from the woods....

"...we had to run for our lives to the shelter of the [river] bank....The river... bounded one side of a large clearing...and we had little fear at first of the fire jumping that space....But we little knew our enemy. [Suddenly] a literal wave of fire over a hundred feet [30 m] high came rolling through the woods....[It] reared its awful crest for a moment towards heaven and then swept like lightning in huge tongues of flame across the clearing.

"'Into the river!' was the yell but before we could plunge down the steep bank ten feet [3 m] and wade in the water up to our necks, the fire had rushed over our heads and the trees on the other side of the stream were all ablaze....

"[As we were] sheltered by a ten-foot [3 m] bank, the body of the flames passed over our heads, making for an hour, an almost solid ceiling of fire....But when a whirlwind of flame, heat, and cinders would [swirl] around our heads ...there was but one escape from death and that was to duck under water and stay till compelled to come up to catch a breath, and often it was only to find the air hotter and more terrible than before.

"As I had rushed down the bank, Clark's baby lay in my path and I picked it up....I am a 'bachelor forlorn,' rather averse to tending other people's babies and Heaven only knows what made me assume the care of that one. But there it was and we had only one old Scotch cap between us to breathe through. I put the cap over the baby's face and pressed my own face to the outside of the cap, and with Heaven's aid that old cap saved two lives. The child was not a year old, but it thought I was trying to murder it and it fought for its life with all its strength. It would place its little feet against my breast and push away from me with all its force, all the time trying to pull the cap from its face. Its light, fine hair was on fire time and time again and we had to duck continually.

"...there was but one escape from death and that was to duck under water and stay till compelled to come up to catch a breath...."

Many residents of Peshtigo instinctively headed for the river, hoping desperately to save themselves from the fire.

After once or twice it would seem to know when we were going down and would hold its breath like an adult—but when above water it kept up a furious screeching continually. I soon made up my mind that there was little hope of getting through alive.... I was chilled through with cold and at last was taken so severely with a cramp in my foot that I could not stand. With the aid of a log...I crawled toward the shore and lay down in the water with my head resting on the bank and the babe beside me, keeping our heads wet by throwing water with my hands. It seemed merely a question of time but in reality I had <u>hope</u> and the babe gave me courage." [2]

About 750 people died in the Peshtigo inferno alone and an estimated 1,500 perished in the entire region. However, on the same night that the Great Peshtigo Fire roared through the Wisconsin woods, the Great Chicago Fire blazed nearly 250 miles (400 km) to the south. The Chicago fire captured the headlines and a larger place in history books, but the Great Peshtigo Fire killed five times as many people.

The Great Flash Flood of Big Thompson Canyon

Big Thompson Canyon in Colorado is a narrow, 25-mile-long (40 km) gorge. It is surrounded by steep, rugged mountains that form part of the Front Range of the Rocky Mountains. U.S. Highway 34 winds its way through the picturesque canyon, linking the city of Loveland, on the Great Plains, to Estes Park, a town cradled at the foot of Rocky Mountain National Park.

Highway 34 runs alongside the Big Thompson River. Much of the canyon is so narrow there is room only for the road and the river. Where the canyon widens, cabins, motels, and campgrounds abound. On the evening of July 31, 1976, about 2,000 to 3,000 visitors

The disaster in Big Thompson Canyon killed 145 people. These dazed survivors head out of the canyon on what was left of Highway 34.

CHAPTER 3

The main road in the canyon "just disappeared," as shown by this aerial photo. Nearly 2 miles (3 km) of U.S. 34 washed away in the flood.

and summer residents filled these motels, cabins, and campgrounds. Few of the vacationers could have anticipated the meteorological events taking place high overhead.

Thunderstorms hunkered down above the mountains near the head of the canyon. Within a four-hour period the storms dumped between 10 and 12 inches (25 to 30 cm) of rain. The water tumbled down the steep, rocky slopes of the mountains. Gullies and ravines, usually dry in summer, turned into raging torrents. These torrents surged into the Big Thompson River, and transformed it into a wild, swollen river. In the narrow canyon the river spilled over its banks and quickly rose 19 feet (5.8 m) above its normal height. It was a classic flash flood.

The Colorado State Patrol and local sheriff departments sent officers into the canyon to warn residents and visitors of the coming flood. No rain had fallen in most of the canyon, so many people ignored the warning. They did not believe themselves to be in danger. There was not enough time for the State Patrol to cover the entire canyon. So some people received no warning at all.

John Lippert, then 20, was a deputy sheriff with the emergency services division of Larimer County, Colorado. Off duty on the night of the flood, he was driving up Big Thompson Canyon to Estes Park with his girlfriend, Cindy: "Cindy and I had been camping in another part of the mountains 30 miles [48 km] away. We had noticed awesome thunderheads building up since early morning. A cloud buildup starting early in the day was quite unusual, but I didn't realize the implications.

"Around 6:30 that evening as Cindy and I headed up Big Thompson Canyon, the sky turned pitch black and it began to rain. We were about 1 mile [1.6 km] east of the tiny village of Drake. The rain pounded down so hard that the windshield wipers couldn't keep up. Still, I thought it was just another downpour. The intensity of the lightning, however, was unusual.

"We traveled another mile [1.6 km] and I noticed that mud and rocks were beginning to slide off the sides of the mountain onto the road. We were one of many cars in a whole string going our way. About 3 miles [5 km] above Drake, I pulled over to the side of the road to wait out the storm. But I became uneasy. My instincts told me to move on, that this was not a safe place.

"So I drove 1 more mile [1.6 km] until we came to a line of cars stopped behind a large motor home on a little rise in the road. By now, in addition to rocks and mud cascading down the canyon walls, trees and boulders 2 feet [0.6 m] in diameter were slipping down, too, and falling on the road. Lightning flashes illuminated the area and I noticed that the Big Thompson River was just a foot [less than a meter] below the shoulder of the road.

"I knew that if the water rose much higher we would have to abandon the car. Five minutes later I saw a family of four running toward us. Their small motor home, 200 yards [182 m] ahead of us, was floating down the road and into the river. Then I knew we were in trouble. The two boys took shelter in our car and their parents went into someone else's.

"The water rose rapidly and I realized that our only option was to climb the mountain. There were 73 of us trapped in this spot, almost all were tourists from out of state. The ages ranged from 8 or so up to 65, but young as I was, I knew I needed to assume leadership. So I started the exodus. Holding on to my girlfriend with one hand—she was leading the two boys—and helping a 50-ish lady with the other, I scrambled 20 feet [6 m] up the side of the mountain to a large outcropping.

> "Drenched to the skin, we clung to the mountainside and watched the river's tirade. My worst fear was that we were going to be struck by lightning."

"It was now around 8:30 PM. Rain was coming down in buckets. Lightning was flashing all around. Rocks, trees, and boulders were toppling off the mountain, and the angry river was rising rapidly. Drenched to the skin, we clung to the mountainside and watched the river's tirade. My worst fear was that we were going to be struck by lightning."[1]

As the storm raged, the river rose and overwhelmed the road beside it. Like John Lippert, Steve Mason, age 22, was trapped near Drake and sought refuge on the mountainside. Years later he shared his memories with a reporter from the *Coloradoan*, a newspaper in Fort Collins, Colorado: "I saw a Winnebago go by with people in it. I saw two or three automobiles go by with people in them. They were screaming and hollering for help, but there was nothing you could do....

"You could barely see anything. You could hear the loud roar of the water and all the noise—all the trees breaking, the banging of the automobiles, the people screaming and hollering and the people crying....

"There was nothing you could really do to help some of those people. If you tried you could lose your own life."[2]

Paul Baker, a trained firefighter and diver with the Loveland Fire Department, was in a better position to help others. A newspaper article in the *Loveland Daily Reporter-Herald* described how he rescued a woman from certain death:

"...there had been reports of a woman stuck in the middle of the water, clinging to a tree and other debris in the middle of the flood. She was stuck...near Big Thompson Elementary School. Baker and another volunteer boarded an Army helicopter and quickly found the woman, who had been swept from a car on a bridge upstream.

"Baker, already in dive gear, told the pilot to get closer to the water.

A forest service worker surveys the incredible destruction caused by the flood. This section of the roadway led from Estes Park to Drake, Colorado.

"'He looked at me and said he'd done some stupid things in his life but what I was about to do was just plumb crazy,' Baker said.

"The 24-year-old volunteer firefighter paid no heed, and plopped into the roaring current, which was full of wrecked automobiles, garbage, homes, and hissing propane tanks. The water quickly carried him to the tree that Melanie Ahlquist, who had lost everything but her bra and contact lenses to the water, was using her last bit of strength to cling to.

"Baker did the appropriate thing. Amid the biggest natural disaster in state history, he introduced himself.... [Then] he laid out a plan to her in plain terms: 'You can either stay here or you can come with me,' he said.

"The choice was not difficult. Ahlquist was harnessed and pulled out by helicopter, then taken to [a hospital]."[3]

IN MEMORY OF TWO GALLANT
LAW ENFORCEMENT OFFICERS

COLORADO STATE PATROL
SGT. W. HUGH PURDY

ESTES PARK PATROLMAN
MICHEL O. CONLEY

THEY GAVE THEIR LIVES TO SAVE THE LIVES OF OTHERS
THE NIGHT OF JULY 31, 1976 WHEN MORE THAN 140 PERSONS
DIED IN THE GREAT FLASH FLOOD OF BIG THOMPSON CANYON.

"LORD OF HOSTS PROTECT US YET
LEST WE FORGET...LEST WE FORGET."

ERECTED BY THE GRATEFUL CITIZENS OF COLORADO
DEDICATED 7-31-78

This memorial plaque commemorates officers Hugh Purdy and Michel O. Conley, who died during the flood. Numerous firefighters and police officers risked their lives to save others during the emergency.

That same night Baker also saved a 14-year-old boy who was clinging to a branch near the same elementary school.

Sheriff's Captain Terry Urista of Loveland, Colorado, was another hero. Like a modern-day Paul Revere, he risked his own life to warn others. Around nightfall, Urista had received a call from his dispatcher, asking him to investigate reports of flooding and to warn people downstream. Urista was incredulous. He lived near the mouth of the canyon and not one drop of rain had fallen there. A newspaper article in the *Loveland Daily Reporter-Herald* described what happened next:

"[Urista] had been barbecuing with his neighbors, his wife, and two young sons, and from his home he could not see the 62,000-foot-high [18,800 m] storm stalled over the Crosier Mountain area.

"When people downstream he was trying to warn did not believe a flood was coming...Urista could only move on."

Near the beginning of the canyon is the Narrows, a 2-mile-long (3 km) stretch with 500-feet-high (152 m) perpendicular walls. According to the *Loveland Daily Reporter-*

Herald: "As Urista drove through the Narrows, he noticed the water appeared roily with a lot of bark, pinecones, and other debris, but that was not unusual if there was a storm. In the darkness he passed through Cedar Cove and came around a curve....

"'All of a sudden the road was gone,' he said....

"Cars were floating by, and 5,000-gallon [19,000 L] propane tanks whistled, gurgled, then whistled some more as they floated past.

"As he traveled back toward Cedar Cove, he saw an A-frame house sitting on a bridge.

"Urista tried to cross an old wooden bridge to get to the people on the other side. As he started across the bridge, he saw a huge pine tree coming toward it. Urista jammed the patrol car into reverse. The tree took out the bridge just as he got off."

Urista tried to contact people and assist as many as possible, but a time came when there wasn't anything else he could do. He spent the rest of the night in his patrol car listening to the other dramas unfolding.

"In one, he remembers listening as deputies tried to assist a man near Loveland hanging in a tree. The deputies were unable to get a rope to him. The man told his son: 'Tell your mother I love her; I can't hang on any more,' and he let go."[4]

After three hours the flood finally subsided. Near Drake, John Lippert left his mountainside perch along with his girlfriend and most of the other stranded motorists. He recalled: "Miraculously our cars had been spared. The large motor home in front of the line of cars had served as a barrier, deflecting the current around the rest of the vehicles. Almost everybody settled back in their own cars, except for one nervous family who didn't come down from the mountains until much later.

> **"I discovered that the road had been washed out in front and in back of us."**

"I had a survival kit in my car so I changed into dry clothes and went exploring. I discovered that the road had been washed out in front and in back of us. The river, still flowing rapidly, whisked three bodies past me."[5]

The Big Thompson Canyon Flood claimed 145 lives. During the next two days, rescue helicopters and jeeps plucked nearly a thousand survivors from the canyon. In the days and weeks that followed disaster crews were able to find all but six of the victims' bodies.

The Big Thompson Canyon will flood again. Signs posted in the area tell travelers to "Climb to safety," a lesson learned by those who survived the flash flood of 1976.

The Big Thompson River will flood again. To prevent loss of lives, several measures have been instituted. The National Weather Service has enhanced its detection and warning system for the region. The road has been elevated and bridges have been built that are designed to resist flooding. In addition, warning signs have been posted in the canyon advising motorists to climb to safety in case of a flash flood. Nevertheless, safety planners worry that people will be reluctant to abandon their cars during a flood. They wonder how they can convince motorists that they are better off wet than dead.

Conclusion

As the twentieth century drew to a close, the United States experienced some notable natural disasters. Hurricane Andrew devastated southern Florida, monstrous floods inundated the Midwest, and the Northridge Earthquake rocked Los Angeles. Even more destructive natural disasters struck outside America's borders. Kobe, Japan, and western Turkey were crumpled by earthquakes. Hurricane Mitch ravaged much of Central America. A tsunami took as many as 3,000 lives in New Guinea. And a monumental eruption of Mount Pinatubo in the Philippines terrorized the half million people who made their homes on the volcano's slopes.

As destructive as they were, these disasters were not unusual in the long history of our planet. In any hundred-year span, Earth may experience about ten million thunderstorms; hundreds of thousands of earthquakes, wildfires, and tornadoes; and thousands of hurricanes, droughts, tsunamis, and volcanic eruptions. Their impact on human populations, and our ability to provide rescue and relief assistance, will determine which of these events will be catastrophes.

Although scientists have not yet found a way to prevent natural disasters, their efforts can help to minimize the toll in human suffering. In Hawaii, for instance, tsunami alerts can save lives—when the alerts are heeded. In volcanic zones, equipment that detects the movement of magma can be used to warn residents about impending eruptions. And storm warning systems, based on satellites and Doppler radar, can alert inhabitants of a region that severe weather is on the way. Our ability to predict severe earthquakes must be greatly improved, though, if we are to defend ourselves against these disasters.

While early warning systems may protect people, they cannot protect buildings—especially those built in areas where some kind of disaster risk exists. Strict building codes are our best defense against future earthquake and hurricane damage to property. Issued by state and local governments, building codes set safety standards that new buildings must meet. To protect both people *and* property, citizens can encourage the passage and enforcement of tough building codes. In the wake of Hurricane Andrew, Florida zoning boards took a close look at how best to build homes and businesses that would withstand a hurricane's fury in the future.

Zoning regulations can provide disaster protection as well, by discouraging developers from building on known earthquake faults, in flood-prone regions, or in coastal areas at risk for tsunamis or hurricane surges. Following the tremendous Midwest floods of 1993, many homeowners and business owners took great care to rebuild safely outside the floodplains of the rivers that ran wild that year.

For their own protection, citizens must insist that emergency response programs in their towns and cities are kept up-to-date. Safeguards for critical transportation systems, telecommunications, and utilities must be regularly reviewed and updated. These services are essential elements of daily life. In the event of a disaster, they are crucial to rescue, relief, and recovery.

Government agencies, corporations, and public service organizations often prepare for future emergencies by:

- training search and rescue teams, including elite K-9 search units
- giving workers, students, and other citizens first-aid training, fire suppression training, and an understanding of emergency procedures so they can respond effectively in a crisis
- establishing or updating evacuation plans
- evaluating methods to keep roads clear in order to ensure that rescue crews can go where they are needed and emergency supplies can be brought in from outside the area.

You are not too young to find out what natural disasters may strike where you live, and what precautions you and your family need to take. Talk to your parents, guardians, or teachers. Every family should have a plan for coping with the natural disasters that are known to occur in their region of the country. At the very least, make sure that your home is equipped with a first- aid kit, flashlight, portable radio, bottled water, canned food, and fresh batteries. Check these supplies regularly.

Perhaps most importantly, we must be aware of disasters which have happened in the past. Communities tend to rebuild quickly after a calamity, and a couple of generations later, few people may remember it. For example, in 1755, a powerful earthquake rocked eastern Massachusetts, and was strong enough to be felt as far away as South Carolina. In Boston, the quake toppled chimneys and clogged streets with rubble. Today, most Bostonians have no knowledge of this quake and are oblivious to the threat of future ones. Yet, the Boston area is at high risk for earthquakes. If Boston were to experience a temblor nearly as powerful as the Northridge Earthquake, the quake damage could be more severe than in California, where strict earthquake building standards have been in effect for some time.

The eyewitness accounts in this book provide exciting reading about real life-and-death struggles against the power of nature. You can learn important lessons from these glimpses into the past—lessons about protecting yourself in the future. After all, you don't want to wind up as a statistic in the next book written by the "Queen of Natural Disasters"!

Source Notes

Ibid. is an abbreviation for a Latin word that means "in the same place."

THE GREAT SAN FRANCISCO EARTHQUAKE

[1] Excerpted from "An Account of the 1906 San Francisco Earthquake," by W.E. Alexander, an undated typed manuscript sent to his cousin, Edwin E. Watts; MS 3456, California Historical Society, San Francisco, CA.

[2] Excerpted from a letter written by Carrie A. Mangels to her uncle John, July 20, 1906; MS 3490, California Historical Society, San Francisco, CA.

ALASKA'S GOOD FRIDAY EARTHQUAKE

[1] Telephone interview on October 22, 1997, followed by e-mail correspondence.

[2] E-mail correspondence, December 1997.

[3] Telephone interview on November 24, 1997.

TSUNAMIS

[1] Telephone interview on September 3, 1997.

[2] Evelyn Miyashiro was interviewed by her daughter Gloria Miyashiro Kobayashi, who then communicated with the author via e-mail, August 1998.

[3] E-mail communication, August 1998.

THE DAY MOUNT ST. HELENS BLEW ITS TOP

[1] Telephone interview on September 18, 1997, followed by e-mail correspondence.

[2] Edited selection from "The Day of the Devil's Snow," an unpublished account by Lu and Mike Moore, 1980.

THE 1900 GALVESTON HURRICANE

[1] Excerpted from *When the Heavens Frowned,* by Dr. Joseph L. Cline; Dallas: Mathis, Van Nort Co., 1946, p. 49.

[2] Excerpted from *Storms, Floods, and Sunshine,* by Isaac Monroe Cline; New Orleans: Pelican Publishing Co., 1945, p. 93.

[3] Ibid., p. 94.

4 Ibid., pp. 95–96.

5 *When the Heavens Frowned,* p. 54.

6 *Storm, Floods, and Sunshine,* pp. 96–97.

7 *When the Heavens Frowned,* pp. 56–59.

8 Ibid., pp. 59–61.

THE NEW ENGLAND HURRICANE OF 1938

1 Excerpted from "Memories of Edith Anderson of Providence," an interview recorded and transcribed in 1989 by Donald West for a college class. In the Albert T. Klyberg Papers, the Rhode Island Historical Society, Providence, RI.

2 Ibid.

3 Excerpted from "True Tales of the Rails: Actual Happenings Told by Eye Witnesses: New England Hurricane," by Harry W. Easton, *Railroad Magazine,* July 1942, pp. 75–79.

THE 1925 TRI-STATE TORNADO

1 Excerpted from "The Deadliest Tornado in American History," *Literary Digest,* April 4, 1925, p. 53.

2 Telephone interview on May 1, 1998.

3 Telephone interview on May 1, 1998.

4 Telephone interview on May 1, 1998.

A PLAGUE OF TORNADOES: THE 1974 TORNADO OUTBREAK

1 Telephone interview on October 27, 1997, followed by written correspondence.

THE BLIZZARD OF 1888

1 Excerpted from a letter by Katherine Ward Fisher of Washington, DC, dated March 12, 1932; From the BV Blizzardmen of 1888 Collection in the New-York Historical Society, New York, NY.

2 *New York in the Blizzard: Being an Authentic and Comprehensive Recital of the Circumstances and Conditions Which Surrounded the Metropolis in the Great Storm of March 12, 1888,* a pamphlet compiled six days after the blizzard by Napoleon Augustus Jennings and McC. Lingan of the *New York Evening Sun* (New York: Rogers & Sherwood, 1888). It contained carefully selected columns of the *New York Evening Sun.*

3 Ibid.

[4] Excerpted from a letter by Milton Daub of New York City, dated March 12, 1944; from the BV Blizzardmen of 1888 Collection in the New-York Historical Society.

[5] *New York in the Blizzard.*

THE BUFFALO BLIZZARD OF 1977

[1] Telephone interview on November 11, 1997, followed by communication via fax.

[2] Telephone interview on December 12, 1997, followed by communication via fax.

DROUGHT IN THE NATION'S BREADBASKET: THE DUST BOWL

[1] "'Dust to Eat': A Document from the Dust Bowl," by Caroline A. Henderson, written in 1935, and edited by Virginia C. Purdy. It was published in *The Chronicles of Oklahoma*, Vol. LVIII, winter 1980–1981, No. 4, edited by Dr. Bob L. Blackburn.

THE GREAT PESHTIGO FIRE

[1] Excerpted from *The Finger of God Is There!, or Thrilling Episode of a Strange Event Related by an Eye-Witness, Rev. P. Pernin, United States Missionary, Published with the Approbation of His Lordship, the Bishop of Montreal* (Montreal, 1874). Reprinted in "The Great Peshtigo Fire," by Rev. Peter Pernin, *Wisconsin Magazine of History*, 54:24–272 (Summer 1971).

[2] Excerpted from "A Terrible Reminiscence: A Night of Horror and a Flight for Life," a handwritten account of the Peshtigo Fire by Elbridge West Meirele, from the Josephine A. Ingalls Sawyer Papers, MAD 4/14/sc 908, State Historical Society of Wisconsin, Madison, WI.

THE GREAT FLASH FLOOD OF BIG THOMPSON CANYON

[1] Telephone interview on May 29, 1998.

[2] Excerpted from "Survivor Recalls People Frozen with Fear," by Dina Cowan in the "After the Flood" feature in *The Coloradoan*, a newspaper in Fort Collins, CO; July 30, 1986, p.10.

[3] Excerpted from "Not All Heroes Are Cowboys," by John Grauberger in the *Loveland Daily Reporter-Herald*, a newspaper in Loveland, CO, July 31, 1996, p. 8.

[4] Excerpted from "The Flood," by Bill McCarthy in the *Loveland Daily Reporter-Herald*, Loveland, CO, July 31, 1991, p. 11.

[5] Telephone interview on May 29, 1998.

Additional Information on Natural Disasters

Listed in Order of Presentation in This Book

MAGAZINE ARTICLES:

"Earthquake: Prelude to the Big One," by Thomas Y. Canby, *National Geographic,* May 1990, pp. 76–105.

"On a Peaceful Good Friday Alaskans Feel the Dread Earthquake!" by William P. E. Graves, *National Geographic,* July 1964, pp. 112–141.

"An Alaskan Family's Night of Terror," by Tay Pryor Thomas, *National Geographic,* July 1964, pp. 142–154.

"Galveston, September 8, 1900: When the Hurricane Struck," by John Edward Weems, *American Heritage,* October 1968, Vol. XIX, No. 6, pp. 36–77.

"The Great Blizzard of '88," by Nat Brandt, *American Heritage,* February 1977, Vol. 28, No. 2, pp. 33–41.

"Tornado," by John M. Schofield and Howard E. Ralinson, *American Heritage,* February–March 1995, Vol. 46, No. 1, pp. 42–46.

"The Great Peshtigo Fire," by Rev. Peter Pernin, *Wisconsin Stories,* a pamphlet reprinted from the *Wisconsin Magazine of History* (Madison, WI: State Historical Society of Wisconsin, 1971).

BOOKS:

Shock Waves Through Los Angeles: The Northridge Earthquake, by Carole G. Vogel (Little, Brown & Co., Boston, 1996).

Volcano: The Eruption and Healing of Mount St. Helens, by Patricia Lauber (Bradbury Press, New York, 1986).

A Disaster Book: Tidal Wave, by Christopher Lampton (Millbrook Press, Brookfield, CT, 1992).

April Fool's . . . the Laupahoehoe Tragedy of 1946: An Oral History, by the students of the Laupahoehoe School (Obun Hawaii, Hawaii, 1997).

Hurricanes: Earth's Mightiest Storms, by Patricia Lauber (Scholastic, New York, 1996).

Weather Eye, by Lesley Howarth (Candlewick, Cambridge, MA, 1995).

Eye of the Storm: Chasing Storms with Warren Faidley, by Stephen Kramer (Putnam, New York, 1997).

Nature's Disasters: Tornado!, by Jules Archer (Crestwood House, New York, 1991).

When Disaster Strikes: Blizzards, by Steven Otfinoski (Twenty-First Century Books, New York, 1994).

The Great Yellowstone Fire, by Carole G. Vogel and Kathryn A. Goldner (Sierra Club/Little Brown, Boston, 1990).

The Great Midwest Flood, by Carole G. Vogel (Little, Brown & Co., Boston, 1995).

WEB SITES:

Earthquakes, Volcanoes, and Tsunamis

U.S. Geological Survey Web Sites

The Great 1906 San Francisco Earthquake
http://quake.wr.usgs.gov/more/1906

Recent Earthquakes in California
http://quake.wr.usgs.gov/recenteqs

Cascades Volcano Observatory's Mount St. Helens Web Site
http://vulcan.wr.usgs.gov/Volcanoes/MSH/framework.html

Cascades Volcano Observatory's Volcano Hazards Web Site
http://vulcan.wr.usgs.gov/Hazards/framework.html

NASA's Observatorium, a Web Site for Earth and Space Information

Tsunami: The Big Wave
http://observe.ivv.nasa.gov/nasa/exhibits/tsunami/tsun_bay.html

Hurricanes, Tornadoes, Blizzards, and Floods

Weather Channel Sites

Historic Hurricanes with Links to Hurricane Safety Tips
http://www.weather.com/breaking_weather/encyclopedia/tropical/history.html

Historic Tornadoes with Links to Tornado Safety Tips
http://www.weather.com/breaking_weather/encyclopedia/tornado

Historic Winter Storms with Links to Winter Safety Tips
http://www.weather.com/breaking_weather/encyclopedia/winter

Historic Floods and Flood Safety Tips
http://www.weather.com/breaking_weather/encyclopedia/flood

Miami Museum of Science Web Site

Hurricane: Storm Science
http://www.miamisci.org/hurricane

Drought and Fire

The Discovery Channel Online

"The Day of the Black Blizzard"
http://www.discovery.com/area/history/dustbowl/dustbowlopener.html

Wind Erosion Research Unit, U.S. Department of Agriculture, Kansas State University

"The Dust Bowl"
http://www.usd.edu/anth/epa/dust.html

Wisconsin Electronic Reader

Rev. Peter Pernin's Complete Account of the Great Peshtigo Fire Online
http://www.library.wisc.edu/etext/wireader/WER2002-0.html

Disaster Preparedness

Federal Emergency Management Agency (FEMA)

How to Prepare for a Disaster
http://www.fema.gov/pte/prep.htm

U.S. Geological Survey and the Southern California Earthquake Center in Cooperation with FEMA and the California Governor's Office of Emergency Services

Putting Down Roots in Earthquake Country
http://www.scecdc.scec.org/eqcountry.html

Humboldt Earthquake Education Center of Humboldt State University, Arcata, CA

On Shaky Ground: Living with Earthquakes on the North Coast
http://glinda.cnrs.humboldt.edu/earthquakes/shaky_ground.html

Acknowledgments

I would like to give my heartfelt thanks to the following people for sharing their stories: Jerry Aqualina, Anne Thomas Donaghy, Jim Gottstein, James Howard, Gloria Miyashiro Kobayashi, John Lippert, Bob Lloyd, Mary Belle Melvin, Evelyn Miyashiro, Mike Moore, Betty Nelson, Leonie Kawaihona Poy, Larry Ramunno, Keith Ronnholm, Jay Smith, Dave Thomas, and Gladys Whipkey.

I am especially grateful to the following individuals for their capable assistance with research: Chris Bauermeister for finding firsthand accounts of the 1906 San Francisco Earthquake; Christine Valentine for tracking down Blizzard of 1888 stories; Rich Stattler, manuscripts curator of the Rhode Island Historical Society Library; librarian Mary Thatcher and assistant librarian Scotty Breed of the Stonington, Connecticut, Historical Society for help with the 1938 New England Hurricane testimonies; Shelly Henley Kelly, assistant archivist of the Rosenberg Library in Galveston, Texas, for assistance with the 1906 Galveston Hurricane accounts; Catherine Ostlind for finding Great Peshtigo Fire descriptions; and Michael W. Lovegrove, archivist, the Carl Albert Center, the University of Oklahoma, for sending me a magnificent account of the Dust Bowl.

Special thanks to the following people for their assistance: Patricia L. Keats, California Historical Society, San Francisco, California; Juanita Cisneros, news librarian, the *Loveland Daily Reporter-Herald*, Loveland, Colorado; Peter Haas, senior editor, State Historical Society of Wisconsin, Madison, Wisconsin; Dr. Walter C. Dudley and Min Lee, authors of *Tsunami!*, published by the University of Hawaii Press; Donna Kellogg, librarian, Loveland Public Library, Loveland, Colorado.

I would also like to acknowledge the help of dozens of other people who took time from their busy schedules to answer questions and refer me to others, especially Louann Kimura of the Laupahoehoe School on the Big Island of Hawaii, and archivist Diane Brenner of the Anchorage Museum of History and Art, Anchorage, Alaska.

I am, as always, indebted to fellow writers Florence Harris, Joyce Nettleton, and Susan Sekuler, as well as to my husband Mark A. Vogel, for their excellent advice and support, and to my nephews Dan, Brian, and Adam Butterworth for their superb insights.

Finally, my sincere appreciation to my editor, Virginia Ann Koeth, for having faith in my manuscript and the talent to help me turn it into a book.

Photo Credits

Index

Page numbers in italics indicate photographs.

About the Author

Carole Garbuny Vogel writes nonfiction books for young readers. Known to her friends and family as the "Queen of Natural Disasters," she is the author of many books, including *The Great Midwest Flood, Shock Waves Through Los Angeles: The Northridge Earthquake*, and *Legends of Landforms: Native American Lore and the Geology of the Land*.

Ms. Vogel is the recipient of the Society of Children's Book Writers and Illustrators Anna Cross Giblin nonfiction Work-in-Progress Grant for *Legends of Landforms*. Her book, *Will I Get Breast Cancer? Questions and Answers for Teenage Girls,* was awarded the Joan Fassler Memorial Book Award for excellence in children's literature dealing with health-related issues.

Carole Vogel graduated from Kenyon College with a B.A. in biology and received an M.A.T. in elementary education from the University of Pittsburgh. She taught for five years before becoming a science editor and running her own consulting business. She lives in Lexington, Massachusetts, with her husband and two college-age children. Now that her children are nearly grown, Carole Vogel keeps in touch with her readership by giving author presentations in schools and libraries.